"With remarkable courage and unwavering honesty, Lisa Whittle writes the whole story—and leaves you ravenous for the only wholesome food for souls: Jesus. If you can't stand the pangs of your holeness any longer, pick up this book."

ANN VOSKAMP
Author of *One Thousand Gifts: A Dare to Live Fully Right Where You Are*

"Lisa Whittle gets it. Her history with the church, her passion for Jesus, and her respect for the story come together in this book called *Whole*. As a grandson and a son of a pastor myself, I value this much-needed message. Lisa offers bold truth to people desperate to find God."

CHRIS SEAY
Bestselling author and pastor of Ecclesia Church, Houston, Texas

"[In *Whole*, you] will read about a woman who moved beyond loving the idea of a holy and omnipotent God to personally experiencing and enjoying the presence of that God. . . . I pray that you will allow Lisa's hard-won lessons in transformation and spiritual growth to help you on your journey to wholeness."

From the foreword by **GEORGE BARNA**
Founder of The Barna Group and author of *Futurecast*

D0188493

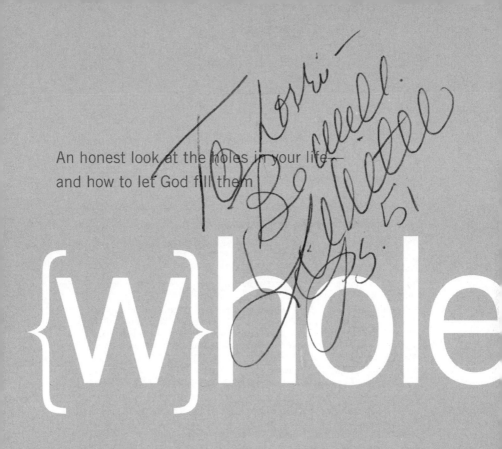

An honest look at the holes in your life—
and how to let God fill them

{w}hole

LISA WHITTLE

Foreword by George Barna

BARNA

AN IMPRINT OF
TYNDALE HOUSE PUBLISHERS, INC.

Tyndale online at www.tyndale.com.

Visit the author online at www.lisawhittle.com.

TYNDALE is a registered trademark of Tyndale House Publishers, Inc.

Barna and the Barna logo are trademarks of George Barna.

BarnaBooks is an imprint of Tyndale House Publishers, Inc.

Whole: An Honest Look at the Holes in Your Life—and How to Let God Fill Them

Copyright © 2011 by Lisa Whittle. All rights reserved.

Designed by Beth Sparkman

Published in association with the literary agency of Esther Fedorkevich, Fedd and Company Inc., P.O. Box 341973, Austin, TX 78734.

Unless otherwise indicated, all Scripture quotations are taken from the *Holy Bible*, New Living Translation, second edition, copyright © 1996, 2004, 2007 by Tyndale House Foundation. (Some quotations may be from the NLT, first edition, copyright © 1996.) Used by permission of Tyndale House Publishers, Inc., Carol Stream, Illinois 60188. All rights reserved.

Scripture quotations marked NIV are taken from the Holy Bible, *New International Version,*® *NIV.*® Copyright © 1973, 1978, 1984, 2011 by Biblica, Inc.™ Used by permission of Zondervan. All rights reserved worldwide. www.zondervan.com.

Scripture quotations marked *The Message* are taken from *The Message* by Eugene H. Peterson, copyright © 1993, 1994, 1995, 1996, 2000, 2001, 2002. Used by permission of NavPress Publishing Group. All rights reserved.

Scripture quotations marked ESV are taken from *The Holy Bible*, English Standard Version® (ESV®), copyright © 2001 by Crossway, a publishing ministry of Good News Publishers. Used by permission. All rights reserved.

Library of Congress Cataloging-in-Publication Data

Whittle, Lisa.
    Whole : an honest look at the holes in your life—and how to let God fill them / Lisa Whittle.
        p. cm.
    Includes bibliographical references (p.   ).
    ISBN 978-1-4143-3798-2 (sc)
1. Christian women—Religious life.   2. Self-realization—Religious aspects— Christianity.   I. Title.   II. Title: Whole.   III. Title: Hole.
    BV4527.W499 2011
    248.8'43—dc23   2011026601

Printed in the United States of America

17   16   15   14   13   12   11
7   6   5   4   3   2   1

To my earthly father, Jim Reimer . . .
who has taught me about grace.

To my heavenly Father, Jesus Christ . . .
who has made my soul well.

Contents

Foreword

One of my favorite expressions is that to a hammer everything looks like a nail. So let me offer the disclaimer that yes, I am a numbers guy. I measure everything and then try to make sense of the outcomes. Given that fact, it may not be surprising that I would posit that Christians in America have a spiritual measurement problem.

Over the three decades that I have been conducting research on faith matters, one of the consistent discoveries has been that we overestimate our own spiritual maturity. We tend to think we're better informed and a lot deeper than we are. It wouldn't be a big deal except that when we give ourselves more credit than is due, such an inflated self-assessment often stands in the way of genuine growth and depth.

In preparation for the writing of Lisa Whittle's book *Whole*, The Barna Group conducted a nationwide survey among a representative sample of 603 women, age 18 or older, who consider themselves to be Christians and are regular church attenders. Ninety-five percent of them say they have made a personal commitment to Jesus Christ that is important in their life, and two-thirds of them can be classified as "born again," based on that commitment and their belief that by confessing their sins and accepting Jesus Christ as their Savior, they will receive eternal salvation.

We learned that Christian women are very comfortable with the state of their faith and spiritual maturity. For instance:

- 81 percent described their relationship with God as "extremely close" or "very close."
- 78 percent are "completely" or "mostly" satisfied with their spiritual development.
- 74 percent said they are mature in their faith.
- 65 percent claimed to be "deeply spiritual."

Really?

It's not my role to judge anyone, but those are some pretty lofty, flattering statistics. What makes me uncomfortable accepting them at face value is that they don't seem to be consistent with some other results that the same survey provided. Jesus said that you will know a person's nature by his or her fruit (Matthew 7:16-20). The survey revealed that the self-assessment of Christian women does not necessarily reflect the fruit of transformed people:

- Only 13 percent said that being a follower of Jesus Christ is the most important role they fulfill.
- Only 16 percent identified their faith as their highest priority in life.
- Only 26 percent listed their top goal in life as something related to their faith or spirituality.

Do you sense a disconnect?

My concern is deepened by the six-year research project I recently completed, an extensive study resulting in a book titled *Maximum Faith*. The study, based on more than fifteen thousand interviews with men and women from across the nation, explores how God transforms people's lives. I should note that less than one out of every twenty-five adults has experienced spiritual brokenness; less than one out of every fifty has surrendered and submitted his or her life to God; and less than one out of every one hundred has a profound, love-driven relationship with God that results in being able to exhibit extraordinary, Christlike love for other people.*

***

*See my book *Maximum Faith* (Ventura, CA: Metaformation and New York, NY: Strategenius Publications, 2011), 17–26.

Additional overtones of dissonance are evident in other research findings. For instance, Lisa and I discovered from the survey undertaken for this book that of eight particular struggles in life that women frequently face, there was not one of those that a majority of women said they "constantly," "frequently," or even "sometimes" struggle with. The list of challenges included such common struggles as envy or jealousy, lust, and arrogance—each of which was said to be a personal challenge by less than one out of every five Christian women!

In a similar vein, the research found that less than one out of every three Christian women in the US admit to wrestling, even "sometimes," with fear, doubt, or confusion. And to be clear about this: previous research I have conducted among men suggests that the same kinds of issues are present among them.

Is it fair to suggest that perhaps we American Christians overestimate our spiritual strength and depth? Is it reasonable to suggest that we are uncomfortable admitting—even to ourselves—that we have significant spiritual struggles and are not as bonded to God as we would like to be? Is transformation so uncommon among Christ followers because we are not willing to do the tough stuff required for us to get over ourselves and hand control of our lives to God, fully trusting Him with every decision and nuance of our existence?

Becoming Whole

The paradoxes identified through research—i.e., the gap between self-perception and behavior—relate to the issue of transformation. Whose values have Christians really embraced: God's or the world's? Which strategy for wholeness is more likely for Christians: the pursuit of daily comfort or the acceptance of situational suffering? What story are Christians most willing and likely to share with others: the orderly, upbeat, happy-ending tale or the narrative of personal brokenness, suffering, and total dedication to Christ?

Lisa Whittle is an unusual Christian, one who is willing to let God determine the trajectory of her life and to work within the parameters He sets for her. That may be the most biblical way of growing, but it certainly is not the most common lifestyle choice. She probably doesn't do it perfectly, but God doesn't expect perfection from us, only consistent obedience.

The research confirms that for the remnant who cooperate with God and allow Him to fully transform them, it is a long, difficult route to follow. It is the same pathway that led to the refining of Paul, David, Moses, and many other heroes of the Christian faith. It is how God works to impassion our hearts, strip us of pride, bolster our trust in Him, reorient our thinking, refocus our attention, and bring peace to our souls. It is not an easy way.

It is the only way.

As you read Lisa's account of how God rerouted her journey, you will encounter the sure signs of someone who has lived the life of the "good, American, Christian woman" only to find that it is a lifestyle infected by social distortions. Thankfully, she has remained attuned to the heart, the voice, the ways, and the will of God, enabling her to recover from a multitude of cultural distortions and distractions that derail our quest for wholeness. You will read about a woman who has moved beyond loving the idea of a holy and omnipotent God to personally experiencing and enjoying the presence of that God. Lisa makes the shift from chasing acceptance by the world to truly seeking only His acceptance. She finally sees through the emptiness of religion and replaces it with the fullness of a significant relationship with God. She recognizes the necessity of dying to self and allowing the Holy Spirit to take control of her being.

The transformation process is not complex, but it is demanding. As Lisa's story will show you, we are not as tough and capable as we think we are, but when we finally surrender to the Spirit of God, we become tough enough to thrive. It takes a determination to allow grace and love to be sufficient in the struggle of daily meaning and purpose. It requires a new self-perception in which our role is no longer that of the strong and independent overcomer, but that of the God-dependent servant.

You and I have holes in our life story that can only be filled by God. When we allow Him to be the center-piece of our life, we transition from a self-made person seeking to transcend the ordinary into an ordinary person capable of doing extraordinary things through the empowerment of God. It's a choice we all face. Too few choose wisely.

I pray that you will allow Lisa's hard-won lessons in transformation and spiritual growth to help you on your journey to wholeness. May her story help you to transi-tion from someone plagued by holes to someone who becomes whole in Christ.

George Barna
JULY 2011

Introduction

THIS BOOK ALMOST DIDN'T HAPPEN.

It was written in its entirety exactly one year ago. And then I threw it in the trash. Something just wasn't right.

I grieved it. I didn't know what to do. God had sidelined me and yet the passion inside of me to deliver the message in this book wouldn't go away.

It was not the only time I was sidelined during the writing of this book. The other came even more inconveniently. In the midst of my second attempt, with the pressure of a looming deadline, I found myself flat on my back in bed in my dark bedroom, staining my down comforter with my tears.

It was right before I wrote chapter 6.

God, what do You want from me? I asked. Only the sound of the natural settlement pops of the house spoke back, so I continued.

I can't write this book without Your help. I don't know what else to say or how to say it. I just want to share my story.

That's when He spoke to my heart.

But what you wrote is not your story, Lisa.

I was taken aback. How could God tell me it wasn't my story when I had lived it, in the flesh? Surely I knew what my story was. I told Him so, in those exact words. My reasoning didn't faze Him, as He continued.

Those are details of your life—your circumstances and experiences. But your real story is what happened between you and Me on the pages of your journey. It's a story you've always had.

At that moment, this book became about more than just the incredible circumstances that happened to me. It became about the whole story: wholeness, the holes within that kept me from it, and the Jesus who made it all complete. It can be your story too. The whole story—the story of wholeness, whereby Jesus fills the voids within that are left in the aftermath of life experiences. It is the wellness of our souls from His healing presence in our lives. It is exactly what we need when we are limited by the gaping holes from our journey—and yet those holes can become exactly the pathway to craving the completion God brings. Our holes may be a necessary part of the journey, but wholeness can become the new story of our life.

I wrote this book because I see a great need among believers. I find us moved by the idea of doing big things for God, but I see life holding us back from it. We have experiences we can't get past. We doubt that God can use us. We don't understand the true purpose of our life outside of the roles we play on an everyday basis. So though we are stirred by pastors, authors, speakers, and leaders to become more for God, we are stifled in that process. As a result, we are a bunch of believers with great intentions that never become the reality we live out.

Whole was written to help position believers better to become the people we were created to be—so that we can serve Jesus the way we were created to do. It addresses the core need of every believer—to become well and whole by the power of God, a step that is often overlooked in our quest for spiritual abundance. I strongly believe that when we are positioned better, our life will show the result.

In the process of recognizing our holes and making the choice to become whole in every area of lack, I believe we will discover our whole story. When we do, we will understand what to share and naturally desire to share it, making an impact on those who occupy space with us in this world. And in case you haven't heard, there is a world full of searching, desperate souls who need what we have in a person named Jesus. They just need us to represent Him well so they will want Him.

A major catalyst for the birth of this book was a book written by my esteemed colleague and friend, George Barna. I read his book *Revolution* right before my husband and I launched a church back in 2009. I underlined nearly every sentence, never having felt more personally understood by a book in my entire life. It thrilled me to realize that after years of playing professional pastor's daughter, stale religion was no longer my god. George's book had painted for me a true picture of what the thriving believer should look like, and finally that picture included me.

In the next few weeks after reading the book, I reflected on what had happened to bring me to such a spiritually thriving place. I wasn't always passionate about God. My choices had often kept me from being well within, even though I had given my heart to Jesus at an early age. My desire to serve Him was often overtaken by the compromises and circumstances of my life.

But finally reaching the point at which I determined I wanted more—more of God, more to life, more of my purpose—I went on a journey to find that *more*. It was then that I was motivated to take an honest look at the inner places where my skewed identity issues and difficult life experiences had limited me . . . and what I

needed to do to have them made whole. In the process,
I found a vibrant new love for Jesus.

That is what I want for you. That is the journey
I pray this book will take you on.

And in the end, after seeing the holes that have held
you back and experiencing the filling of God within
them, you will find the life of the revolutionary. You
will be moved to fulfill a greater purpose. You will be
empowered to share the story of your journey: how you
once lacked in places that He filled . . . once craved what
His hand freely offered . . . and once discovered the fullness of your life in the pages of your whole story.

Lisa Whittle
APRIL 2011

Some of the names in this book have been changed in order to honor the
privacy of those who shared their stories. But all stories have been used with
permission, and they are all completely true.

CHAPTER I

THE HOLE STORY

What seems a hindrance becomes a way.

HENRI NOUWEN

THE TEARS WERE FALLING IN RECORD NUMBER. I hated that I couldn't stop them. But when dams break, things get wet.

I had been to therapy, but this couch session was different. It wasn't a professional with a mahogany-framed degree who sat in front of me; it was my longtime friend, Monty. And he wasn't holding back his assessments.

"You doubt God, Lisa. You doubt what He can do through you."

His words jolted me, not unlike the moment in the

middle of a minor league baseball game just weeks prior when I was hit in the face by a stray baseball: I hadn't seen it coming and I thought, *Oh,* that's *what it feels like.* It's not that I hadn't been confronted with truth before. It's just that as a grown adult, it had been a while, and it hurt more than I had thought it would.

The presence of my husband next to me on Monty's sectional should have made me feel comfortable. Instead, I felt strangely exposed. Monty was a mentor to both of us, and we had been vulnerable with him before. But I didn't want my ugly private thoughts pulled out, being laid bare in front of anyone. The truth is, I still wanted them not to be true. If I didn't give them a platform, maybe they could continue to live behind the curtain.

But Monty had outed them for me, here in his living room, and I couldn't cram them back in. My husband and I had flown across the United States to vacation in a place where we could also spend time with Monty and his wife. But this confrontation was more than I had bargained for, and I found myself wondering if the trip itinerary should be dusted for the fingerprints of God.

My dam broke that day, releasing a flood of tears down onto Monty's corduroy couch. But it was because of much more than my embarrassment from the exposure. I cried ultimately because I knew what he said was true. No matter how much I wanted to deny it, the journey of my life confirmed it: my story was full of holes.

My story: my life . . . my journey . . . the things I'd seen and done in my life. My holes: the things that had come as a result, limiting and defining me. Holes in my religion, roles, and experiences had kept me from many things: effectiveness, peace, fulfilling my created purpose. Some of them I had dealt with before, but others had found a corner of my heart to hide out in, lying dormant until something called them out. Doubt, lurking in the hole that my life experiences had formed, was being forced out into the open. The thought had nagged me for years while I ignored it, but now it had become evident to someone other than me. I wanted God to use me. I just wasn't sure He would.

I wonder if you relate to this feeling of wanting God to use you but not knowing if He ever will. I wonder if you are among the seventy million people who feel like something from your past is holding you back in life.[1] I wonder if, like mine, your story is full of holes— limitations that have gotten in your way or that have been allowed to live behind a curtain or hide out in a corner. I wonder if you know that all of that can change, or if you just think those are words that look good on the page of a book. Most of all I wonder if you know that you have a story to tell at all.

I have been the skeptic who doubted the latter for myself. I have been the good girl, and I have also been the bad. I have searched and found, loved and lost, failed and succeeded. I have been a religious addict—loving the idea of God more than His presence. I have seen Him stay around when others walked away. I have watched Him change the course of my life at a time when it was careening recklessly in a dangerous direction.

I have no reason to doubt. My first instinct was to tell Monty that. After all, the inner religious addict that was overthrown during my spiritual recovery some years back still lurks quietly inside, waiting for moments like this when it can rise up, if I allow it, to muffle truth again with its articulate, saintly manifesto.

But I was weary of that mess—that private place that feared soul exposure. I needed to own up to what Monty said, even though it was painful. I needed to deal with it so that the hole inside no longer had control over me. Throughout my life I had lived both ways, with my holes left unattended on the one hand and with Jesus filling them up on the other. And I knew that the only way my life would be made well was if truth won. Otherwise, I was relegated to a hollow existence— a number holder, occupying space in someone's line. That was something I could not accept.

I don't want you to accept it either. My friend, you

are not meant to live a hollow existence. You are not meant to live life relegated to your holes . . . to be a space occupier, a number holder. You are meant to be a world influencer, a life alterer, a game changer. You are meant to live life well by becoming whole. You are meant to be a storyteller.

This rich promise of your purpose is found in Romans 9:17: "I have appointed you for the very purpose of displaying my power in you and to spread my fame throughout the earth." Jesus wants to take a wrecking ball to the barriers that keep you from your divine appointment to display His power in you. He wants to use your voice to spread His fame. The question is, is this something you want too?

You are meant to be a storyteller.

Dust this page for His fingerprints. They are all over this moment and all over your future . . . in the story . . . of your life.

But I Don't Have a Story

I have always known the power of a story. As the daughter of a pastor, I grew up hearing countless numbers of them told weekly from a wooden pulpit: persuasive, stirring, effective. I waited for them during the sermon every

Sunday, as if they were the ice-cream truck and my sweaty hand were ready with my fifty cents. The stories mattered. I loved them. I needed them to help me make sense of everything else in the finely orated message delivered by my father. I could remember them and often did, well on into the next week . . . the next story . . . the coming years of my life, even when I remembered nothing else.

For a time, I was satisfied with hearing someone else's story. The translated pages of another person's life intrigued me. But at some point, I wasn't satisfied any longer. I suspect it happened right about the time an evangelist in eelskin cowboy boots came to our redbrick church in the heart of a small Oklahoma town.

I don't remember his name, but I remember the color of his hair (sandy brown) and his story (sordid). He'd had four stepfathers—they'd all abused him. He left home at sixteen. Became homeless a year later. Lived in an alleyway. Drank his liver to near failure. Prayed for his life to end.

Of course, it didn't. But there was an ending to the sordid part of his story, and it was glorious. It had to be, I knew, for him to stand on the stage as a preacher. After all, people who got on stages had their lives all together. That's what I thought.

The glorious portion of his story was this: Someone told him about God. He was offered a home and doctored back to health. He got his GED, enrolled in Bible college, and studied to become a minister. His was an amazing story: vibrant, captivating, and neatly tied up with a shiny Jesus bow.

But all I can remember thinking as I sat in the padded pew, a young girl who loved to listen to someone else's story, was, *I don't have a story*. It was as if I knew that the safe, beautiful life God had blessed me with would never be worthy of sharing on a stage. Suddenly, I didn't want to hear someone else's story. I wanted to have one of my own.

Maybe the circumstances of your life have left you in no doubt as to what your story is and you need no convincing that your story is worthy to be shared. Or maybe like me, you have lived your life listening to other people's stories, and there is a place inside that burns to have one of your own: one to know, to share, that's important. No matter the point at which we are on our wholeness journey, we all want our story to matter— to resonate in the heart of another. But first we have to know we have one and that it can make a difference.

I can assure you: you do and it can. Jesus did not create people without stories or without giving their stories purpose. We all have empty places that we need Jesus to fill—even those of us who have already experi- enced the healing presence of God in certain areas of our life, but as life happens, different holes have surfaced. The stories we live are not perfect. They don't have to be tied up in a crisp, shiny bow before we can share them. True, we will never be whole in the most complete sense until we reside in heaven. But based on the promises of Scripture about the joy we can experience on earth, I believe a measure of wholeness is possible in this life. Otherwise our story is just about our holes, and that leaves out Jesus. (And really, who would be compelled by that?) Wholeness through Jesus is a story meant to change the very course of life, starting with your own.

Why Your Story?

There has never been, nor will there ever be, any better storyteller than Jesus. His stories were so powerful that He was not without a captive audience to hear them, and usually that audience was packed full of eager, story-hungry people. This is exactly what happened in Matthew 13, when He spoke to the large crowd from a boat that sat by the populated shore. In the midst of His storytelling, His curious disciples asked Him, "Why do you tell stories?" (verse 10, *The Message*)

Jesus replied in just a few compelling words. "I tell stories: to create readiness, to nudge the people toward receptive insight" (verse 13, *The Message*). He could've rattled off some articulate spiritual manifesto. But instead, He spoke as He always did, with spiritual directive and purpose. Jesus, the great storyteller, said much even in these few words: that stories are important; that they are readiers, movers, prompters of the heart.

Stories level the playing field of human worth. There's no special training needed to share a story. There's no hierarchy of calling. There's no sensationalistic hook required. Just a life that is changed. A willing heart. A passionate soul.

Why *your* story? Because you are the best one to tell it. Because it will create space for Jesus in the hearts of those who hear it. Because it will nudge someone toward receptive insight into their Creator. Because someone else can deliver factual information about the experiences of your life, but only you can be the living, breathing representation of its details. There is no one better to make the name of Jesus—master storyteller, whole-life giver—famous.

Holes in Your Story

Let's be honest: on our journey, things get in the way of wholeness. There are roadblocks to our lives being well. Life is complicated by outside factors we cannot control, and Jesus let us know up front this is the way it would be when He said, "In this world you will have trouble" (John 16:33, NIV). Things we experience on the outside—struggles we have or issues beyond our control, like health problems—can and do compromise our well-being. But these are not holes. Holes happen within. They are voids in our soul. They are the result of things that happen to us on our journey of life.

Often this involves a confusion about religion, our pathway to God—one of the primary places for Satan, the very real enemy of our souls, to succeed at pulling us away from God. If we can be confused by our religion, we can be limited in our faith. In the lives of many believers, holes have been formed through disappointment in the church, feelings of being judged and misunderstood by other believers, or mistrust for ministry leaders who didn't use their leadership well.

Roles are another big creator of holes—the way we see ourselves and decide our worth based on what we do or who we think we are. Even though we know that our true identity is in Jesus, things threaten to skew it, either making us feel insignificant or causing us to feed on pride.

And then there are our experiences. Big. Life altering. Real. In many ways, these troubling outside factors Jesus is referring to in John 16:33 are what can help create some of our deepest holes. But sometimes it will be our own decisions that change our lives in ways that lead us away from what is pure and good. Other times it may be internal beliefs we hold on to that eat away at our soul.

Experiences shape us, and they can create holes. But they don't have to.

Holes take away so much from us. They plunder our vibrant relationship with God. They limit our future and define our past. They prevent us from being well within. They keep us from sharing our whole story.

But with every hole comes an opportunity. In many ways, we need the holes so we will be spurred on to pursue what is better. For every place where we lack the filling of God, He is ready, able, and willing to step in and produce completeness. What was empty, ritualistic religion can become the place where we find a most authentic faith. The role that changes without our permission or makes us feel too important can become the catalyst to make us seek and embrace our true identity. The experiences we gather on the pages of our journey that disrupt, hurt, confuse, and limit us can become the circumstances in which we most see God. So to extend Henri Nouwen's idea, our hindrances produce a way to experience more of our Creator. Holes are not the end of our story. In the wholeness journey, they are truly our beginning.

As Your Journey Begins

Give this moment your full attention.

You can't change what you don't recognize as a problem. Your holes may be giving off signs: discontent, lack of fulfillment, fear, pain, shame, pride, anger . . . and as with me, doubt. Pay attention to those signs, because they may be pointing to a great hole that is keeping you from wholeness, limiting your potential for God. But don't stop there. Recognize that even in the depths of those voids, you are on the cusp of vast opportunity.

In the events of my life, as you will soon read, there was always a choice: to live with the things that limited me or to bring them from behind the curtain to provide a platform for change. Sometimes I chose well; sometimes I didn't. (You have this choice, too, even at this moment.) In the midst of my most incredible experiences, even the most painful, there was a ground-swell of hope that beauty could come from the ashes. It is one of God's greatest gifts to us—the hopeful promise of turning ugly into beautiful—and it is ours, unconditionally.

Sharing my story has been in many ways more diffi-cult than the exposure of my doubt. Those things I expose in the coming pages, about which I have stayed silent for almost twenty years—my prison break from formulized religion, the excruciating loss of a defining role, the soul refinement of painful experiences—have led to my spirit's exhaling the personal testimony that *it is well, it is well with my soul.* I marvel at this today, pray-ing that God will continue this work in my life, keenly aware of my very human capacity to fall away from truth, to compromise my own wholeness.

What about you? Is your soul well? Is anything holding you back from that beautiful place called whole?

I pondered these questions myself in the days after my truthful couch session with Monty. And though I preferred to keep my doubt tucked safely behind the curtain, I knew it needed to be allowed a platform so truth could win. Yes, I was a believer in Jesus. Yes, I had come a long way in my faith. Yes, I knew the Bible and loved my Creator. And yes . . . I was limited by the doubt in my life that He wanted to use my story. That was the truth, and the truth was ugly. Because it wasn't really about doubt at all; the doubt was just a symptom. It was about the hole that held me back from God.

And as I allowed the dam to break over this thought once again, this time in the privacy of my bedroom closet, I told Jesus, *This moment is Yours. Don't hold back. Tell me the whole story.*

And in the way only He can, He held my heart as He reminded me of my journey: of the lost things that He restored . . . of broken places that He fixed . . . of gaping holes that He filled . . . of things that had been sick that He made well . . . of a little girl who finally found her story, the one she had been living all along.

It is what Jesus, the greatest storyteller of all time, wants to show you. Give this moment to Him. Ask Him not to hold back. And then sit expectantly at the shore of hope as He shares with you the details of your whole story.

Questions to Consider

1. Do you believe you have a story? If so, do you understand why God might want you to share it?

2. What is a hole? How have holes held you back in life?

CHAPTER 2

THE HOLE OF RELIGION

Not all people who sound religious are really godly.

MATTHEW 7:21

COMING FACE-TO-FACE with the holes in our life can
feel shocking at first, especially when they have been
pointed out to us in the bold voice of another. Maybe
that's because though loving confrontation should be
a valuable part of living life amidst the body of Christ,
it often isn't, which is a great injustice. Our voids are
allowed to live behind the curtain so long that we are
surprised when they become exposed, as was the case
with my couch session with Monty. But long before that
took place, someone else had the courage and insight to
sprinkle seeds of truth deep into my heart.

The year was 1980-something, and the place was summer church camp. It was a familiar setting for me as the pastor's daughter who attended every event our youth group held with both duty and enthusiasm. I was particularly anticipating camp this year: I was going with a little secret tucked away in my heart, soon to be revealed. For weeks I had been preparing a very special "rock star speech" to impress my fellow campers and leaders with. I loved my crazy-haired, over-caffeinated youth pastor, and I wanted to make him proud of the person he had helped raise up as a leader in the youth group. Most of all, I hoped to make others (even myself) believe what I desperately wanted to be true: that I was passionately in love with Jesus.

Some years before, I had decided that since I was not going to have a remarkable, earth-shattering story to share, one telling how Jesus saved me from a horrific existence, I would have to find something else to make me valuable to the Kingdom. Somewhere in my mind I made the determination that my only way to forge that bond with Jesus and His people was just to do religion really well. It was something I had been practicing for a while, but this year it would reach its culmination. My moment of opportunity would come at the campfire confessional: the sin-purging session that happened every year on the last night of camp.

It was an important night for all of us, not only because we would bond over the glow of the open flame but also because it would represent a week's worth of conviction stirred up by the guest youth speaker flown in for the week. I'd been around long enough to see them come and go—and to find them strangely similar: endearingly goofy, frenetically energetic, and passionately fond of words like *awesome* and *stoked*. Most good budget years, said speaker would get a sidekick in the form of a camp worship leader—which gave me, a girl who loves her music, yet another reason to look forward to camp. By the last campfire, if the students got emotionally jacked up to the point of dramatic confessions and promises of change, this dynamic duo could take it as a sign that they had done their job well.

After years of experience, I knew what to expect. As a full-time pastor's daughter, I had been in the Jesus business for a very long time. The little speech I'd prepared and cherished in my heart was part of a familiar, well-rehearsed game I played. Crying, smiling on cue, and saying just the right words are things not exactly taught but certainly shown by people in the Jesus business, and I was a star pupil of my own observations. I had collected these observations, and it was these that led me to my "confession."

After a fun four days, the last night of camp finally

arrived. I was nervous and expectant. I watched silently as my friends took the mic, one by one, purging their one year's worth of wrongdoing into the crackling amplifier for all to hear. "I haven't been honest with my parents," one crying girl said. "I need to have a quiet time," said another. And the ever-popular, highly inspirational, "I want to win my school for Christ!" as cool kids who had previously shied away from associating with church became suddenly passionate about becoming evangelistic. I was almost up, and my palms were growing sweaty.

The moment arrived, and I was up at the mic. I cleared my throat and spoke loudly: "I want to live my life this year for God so that I don't have to come back here and confess next year all the things I have done wrong. I'm tired of living for myself, and I want to live for God this year like never before!"

That was it. My moment had been brief, but I felt its impact—in my own mind, anyway. My imagination had the group of campers suddenly morphing into thousands of cheering fans. I had managed to amaze even myself. Somehow, in between years and years of flyswatting my way through the morning devotionals at camp and sweating my way through the dreaded afternoon athletic activities, I had managed to fake my way through yet another campfire confessional. Though I had never gone to these lengths, deep down I knew most of my moments like these were insincere. I could tell I had knocked it out of the park this time by the approving look on my youth pastor's face. He loved what I had said, I could see that. And I loved myself because he'd loved it so much. I had gloriously pulled it off.

I let my success soak in, enjoying the hugs and smiles from proud leaders and supportive friends, eventually watching the campfire area clear and the imaginary legion of adoring fans disperse to their cabins. Just as I was moving to join them, I felt a large, calloused hand on my shoulder.

"Come over here," someone said. "I want to talk to you for a minute."

I turned around. It was the worship leader—not a face I was expecting to see looking back at me, especially since he was just a guest, flown in from another state, and he didn't really know me at all.

I acquiesced, feeling like I didn't have much choice. But I had already started formulating my thoughts around the best spiritual answer I could give for whatever I had done, not done, or thought about doing (I was sure I was guilty of that much, at least). Whatever was going to get me out of there and back behind a tree to go to first base with my boyfriend was exactly what I would do.

The worship leader's eyes were big and round, expressive and penetrating. To be honest, they made me nervous. I saw purpose behind his stare as he said this: "Lisa, I see something in you. Right now, I can tell you are playing the game and not being sincere about your love for God. But I believe you have great potential for the Kingdom. I am not here to condemn you or tell you what you are doing wrong. I'm here to challenge you to pursue God and live your life better. You play your part well, but you are destined for so much more."

He may have said something else; I can't remember. I don't even remember walking off after he gave the speech. All I can recall is making my way down a dusty path, back to my cabin, with a wet face, soaked by snot and tears. My boyfriend was no longer on my agenda.

I just wanted to be alone. My thoughts were a jumble, and I had a gutted feeling in my stomach like nothing I had ever before experienced. On the one hand, I was shocked by his candor. On the other, I was embarrassed he could see through my facade. Most of all, I felt exposed and ashamed. I thought about the truthfulness of his words and how painful they felt when they hit my ears. I thought about the sound of my own voice, sitting around the campfire, saying things about God that I didn't really mean. I thought about the games, the fake-outs, and doing what would spiritually get me ahead.

I thought about Jesus, and I thought about how at this moment, I hated the way my religion made me feel. It was my first experience with what many believers have come to know: religion will always feel bad when we define our relationship with a supreme God by simply trying to perform spiritual things really well.

As I think back on that moment in my life, I am reminded of how deep the hole already was that my religion had created in me, even at this early age. I was so limited by the good-girl formulas and performances that I did not realize that they defined me and kept me from experiencing something real. All I knew was that I didn't feel close to God. It took someone having the courage to speak truth into my life to get me to feel the weight of what was happening inside my heart: religion made me feel empty.

It was not religion itself that was to blame; it was religion written within my parentheses of ritual. The

Religion will always feel bad when we define our relationship with a supreme God by simply trying to perform spiritual things really well.

spiritual appearances, the perfectionism, the misplaced hope to impress and to feel good inside by performing well on the outside—all this defined my religious life to that point, and that is what created the hole. I was young, but I knew enough to recognize that the spiritual component of my life was missing a key element: authenticity.

An authentic faith. Most of us want it, but we don't know how to fully live it. That is why we so often turn to *religion*—which is familiar and comfortable and can easily be defined by rituals we do and things we say. Religion doesn't require deep soul-searching or effort; it even yields short-term results. People are impressed. It produces phantom feelings of closeness to God, if only for a time. But always, in the end, we wind up feeling empty. Disillusioned. Shamed over presenting a false picture to others as if it were true. Limited in our relationship with God.

Being confronted by a hole that was holding me back was different back in those days of summer camp. I was younger, more naive, and hadn't lived enough life to understand many things about God. But then, as with my moment with Monty, I was affected by truth. The holes were different, but in many ways the tears from both moments felt the same. They were truthful, thoughtful tears. Longing, wishful tears. Tender, regretful tears. My holes had made an impact, and I allowed myself to feel it in order to open the door to change. My masking, covering, and patching efforts hadn't worked. Muting the nagging feelings within no longer quieted

them. To gain true and lasting spiritual freedom, I would
have to be brave enough to look at those holes without
looking away. It would mean the difference in the quality of my very life and how much I would be able to
experience a real God without limits—something I had
always wanted. And something, as it turns out, that is
available to us all.

Becoming Limited

No one ever starts out in life wanting to become limited.
Even people who don't live life driven toward enormous success naturally tend to reject the idea that they
won't be able to get somewhere they want to go in life.
Spiritually, this is no different. The idea that we might
have been feeding our souls with a religion of merely
ritualistic practices empty of actual spiritual life—that it
is our pursuit of religion for its own sake that has ultimately limited or defined us—is a painful one, especially
when we have invested a lot of time and energy in that
pursuit. Some of us refuse even to consider such an idea,
which is why we never experience God in a deeper way.
Others would argue that the traditions of our religion
can be rich, inspiring, and helpful, and certainly—to an
extent—I agree. Many of us "religious" people—that
is, Christians—are able to enjoy our various traditions
without equating them with God. Unfortunately, it's

in our nature to confuse these things sometimes and cause them to spill over, which can create a limiting hole within our soul.

Religion is not to be blamed, although I can admit that sometimes the religious community unknowingly fosters dependence on spiritual acts that are seen. But when religion overshadows relationship with God, something must change. It is not an aversion to the presence of tradition that we must take up but a challenge of the absence of true spiritual vibrancy within it. Only when our religious traditions, and our following of them, define our view of God in a way that is consistent with what He says about Himself in the Bible can our religious traditions function in health.

This is why it is so important to understand that no matter our background or past circumstances, we have a story and that story is significant. One of the biggest catalysts for living a rigid religious existence driven by formulas rather than by the living Spirit of God is desperation for connectedness to Him. In many ways, it is what drove me to perform spiritually for years. We want others to see us as spiritual. We have a need to feel that others believe us to be enthusiastic followers of Jesus. Most of all, we want to have something to offer God. We think that if we give Him enough of our ritual, He will know we love Him. Often, it is how we convince even ourselves. But in the process it creates a hole, which only further drives us away from His heart.

Sometimes the development of this hole involves our attachments—the things we come to depend upon because they remind us of God. Things like our Sunday morning service agenda, and padded pews or theater seating or plastic chairs. Thick wooden pulpits versus modern café tables, and Wednesday night women's Bible studies versus online ones. Our comfortable religious traditions can make us feel spiritually productive, maybe even spiritually complete. But in the process, they can obstruct our view of God. The reality is that though we feel like we are making efforts toward loving Him, we may simply be in love with our religion.

Our spiritual life then becomes the house that's built on sand, devoid of a solid core foundation on the person of Jesus Christ. Matthew 7:24-27 talks about the importance of this:

> *Anyone who listens to my teaching and follows it is wise, like a person who builds a house on solid rock. Though the rain comes in torrents and the floodwaters rise and the winds beat against that house, it won't collapse because it is built on bedrock. But anyone who hears my teaching and doesn't obey it is foolish, like a person who builds a house*

on sand. When the rains and floods come and the winds beat against that house, it will collapse with a mighty crash.

Some of us know this mighty crash of religion. We are familiar with what happens when the spiritual traditions we have built our Christianity upon don't stand up to the winds of difficulty on our journey. We become limited when what we have made God to be proves hollow because it was never built on depth. But even if those winds don't blow hard enough to bring down our spiritual edifices, they still—eventually—prove ineffective.

> *Though we feel like we are making efforts toward loving God, we may simply be in love with our religion.*

Ineffectiveness

If there's one person who understands the ineffectiveness of a stale religion, it's Riley. The first time I talked to her, I knew I rode her wavelength. I had used social media to ask for personal stories from people who had broken out of a traditional religious rut to develop a more thriving relationship with God, and Riley was one of those who responded, inviting me over to her house for coffee and a chance to hear about her journey. She and her family were fairly new to the area, having moved to North Carolina to start a ministry, and we had been introduced previously through a mutual friend. But this was the first time we had ever really had a good, solid talk.

I stepped into her eclectically chic home eager to pick her brain about her experience, knowing that her journey to becoming spiritually authentic could not have been without its challenges. After pouring our coffee, we made our way over to the couch. Almost immediately, Riley began to share. She talked about her strict upbringing and life without her dad. From the ostracism of her parents' divorce to the church discipline she feared after her secret abortion, Riley shared pieces of her journey that had led her down many roads of ritualistic tradition, betrayal, fear, and ultimately forgiveness.

Much of what she said had an impact on me, but one thing in particular stood out. The moment she said it, it resonated somewhere deep within my heart. "As a young woman," she said, "I can remember looking around the church one day at all the plastic women with smiles on their faces, who looked perfect on the outside, and thinking, 'I don't see any one of these women I can relate to. I don't look like them. I'm not like them. I don't want to be like them. If this is what being a Christian is all about, I want no part.'"

Riley's words took me back to my own history with
the church, as I remembered having some of those same
thoughts. My mind then traveled to thoughts of my
twentysomething friends now, and how they view religious people. I've talked with some of them about it, so I
had a pretty good idea. Riley's testimony confirmed what
I have learned about why people—not just women—
don't listen to us believers when we try to speak to them
about spiritual things: they simply don't trust that our
relationship with God is for real. They see our religious
act as a smoke screen. Their view of God through the
lens of our pretense creates within them a spiritual hole,
leaving them to wonder what the truth is. So when we
get face-to-face with them and attempt to speak to them
about Jesus, like Riley they want no part.

I can think of no greater tragedy than to turn people
off to Jesus, though we often do. We are called to
live the authentic gospel to others, but with holes in
our lives, this is just not possible. Though we are not
responsible for the actions of others, we are responsible
for ours. The beautiful result of a faith made whole
is that it provides an example of the attractive life of
Christ which, in turn, creates an appetite for Him.
This may well be the only way some of them will ever
come to God. We know this is His desire for us as
His children. As it says in John 15:8, "This is to my

Father's glory, that you bear much fruit, showing your-selves to be my disciples" (NIV). When we ourselves are devoid of a thriving, authentic relationship with God, we lose the ability to represent Jesus well. Only Jesus can replace synthetic religious hearts with spiritual vibrancy. The emptiness Riley talked about is what it looks like when that doesn't happen.

Our holes prevent us from being believable. Our influence loses its viability, and Jesus becomes merely a legendary figurehead instead of the living, powerful rescuer He truly is. As a result, people are driven away from church for the rest of their lives, leaving them to question whether God is real. More than thirty million adults say that their experiences with religion have caused them to question God.[2] Clearly, religion has a great deal of influence over us and has, for many people, colored the way we view God. When our negative experiences with religion cause us to view God nega-tively, we have made religion itself too important.

But the personal ramifications for us as spiritual examples are significant too. Our holes from empty religion have led to the erosion of our very own hearts. They pull us into a dangerous trap of self-loathing and shame for the ways we know we are not sincere in our faith. We want to love God. We should love God. We don't feel worthy to be loved completely by Someone we only worship when people are looking. That's where the temptations to keep secrets, play games, and give our rock star speeches about God come into play. But all they do is keep us bound to that formula we think we need for connecting ourselves to Him, until the winds come and blow it all away. And eventually . . . they will.

Spiritual Roadkill

Depending on our religion sets us up for failure. We become limited by it and then it holds too much power over us—power to alter all that we believe about God, power to convince us never to darken the doors of a church again. Stephen Mansfield, in his book *ReChurch*, talks about this common reality among people who have been hurt by the church or by a religious leader and the deep consequences it brings. He says, "Here is where we begin to set ourselves up for pain and disillusionment, for in our love for our church and our holy regard for those who lead us in the things of God, we forget the nature of humanity."[3]

Humanity. People being people, including religious people who sometimes behave badly. When religion becomes primary and is allowed to define our spiritual experience, it is given the power to devastate our faith structure because this makes reality with God secondary. It becomes difficult to separate the hurts from the church or leaders or other believers from the character of Jesus, which is often so very different. So not only does a faith built on the sand of religion foster inauthenticity, affect our influence, and shame us for the ways we are insincere, it also produces a platform for rejection of good, solid things like church and community with other believers, maybe even cutting off fellowship with God.

Many of us, more than we may realize, are ourselves lying beside the road of religion we once happily traveled along. Somewhere in the years of our journey with Jesus and with the church, we have felt judged. Ostracized. Thrown away like roadkill on the side of a busy highway. We have become disillusioned by a leader or a pastor or fellow church member who did not handle our heart well. And when they did what humans sometimes do, we were left to believe that no one who occupies a pew or stands on a stage can really be trusted.

Every time I hear a story where someone feels the sting of hypocrisy or dismissal by a religious organization or person of faith, my heart hurts for what may come next: a great questioning of the authenticity of God, traveling down roads of inquisition about His sovereignty and character—core faith issues produced by the hole from an empty religion and the subsequent hurt it cost. The questions are so often the same: "Is God really real? Does He really love me? How do I know I can trust Him?" ˙

I wish I could stop hurtful things from happening in the church. But they just keep happening because people just keep wearing flesh. We are not perfect. We sometimes behave badly. And when we wear spiritual accessories to cover a shallow relationship with God, it can lead to spiritual roadkill—people tossed aside with a soul full of holes. And yet, the side of the road can also be the very place in our life where He can become most real to us.

Moving toward Wholeness in Our Religion

In the midst of our grappling with religion—trying to identify those moments that have developed holes within us and have consequently limited us from a vibrant spiritual life—stands God. Desiring to give us depth. Ready to prove He is more than a formula, solid enough to build our entire spiritual life upon. While we scramble to reconcile with a religion that has limited us, He waits patiently to prove Himself true. His hands reach out in understanding. His arms offer support. His love for the one wounded by a religion that has defined him or her is furious and enveloping. His passion for the soul lying spiritually undeveloped burns strong. He won't run away, no matter how ugly our mess.

There are many like me, people who have spent years of life in religious trappings to prove to ourselves and others that we really love God, but in the end we have proved to be as flimsy as dollar-store decorations when the winds of life blew through. To us He says, *Take off those accessories. This is your moment to make your faith about Me—it's your time to experience something real. The holes that religion has formed inside of you are now going to be your greatest conduits of My love. Let Me prove Myself capable of making you whole.*

To those among us who have lived the experience of being tossed aside like roadkill, gravely disappointed by an aspect of our religion, He says, *You built your faith on sand and it couldn't sustain you. But I love you, and that hasn't changed. Now let's move on together. Get up, dust yourself off, and construct your spirituality on Me, a foundation that can't be compromised.*

Yet others of us—normal, everyday people who drive our kids to sports practice, get involved with ministries, work in coffee shops, own businesses, and volunteer—are not exempt. We have a great need for religion to become less and God to become more so we can represent the person of Jesus well, live in freedom from guilt and pretense, and experience wholeness, the healing of holes formed by settling for the ritual of a common faith instead of the faith itself. To us He says, *Stop convincing yourself you are not in need of more of Me. Realize your need for Me to invade your spiritual space—to fill your religious holes and produce something radical and real.*

In all of these things, it is the beauty of Jesus—the One who "heals the brokenhearted and binds up their wounds" (Psalm 147:3, NIV)—that breathes into the empty holes of shallow, religion-bound believers, filling us up with Him.

Questions to Consider

1. How can dependence on your religious performance limit you? How do you think God views a connection with Him that is based largely on spiritual ritual?

2. Has your religion ever been given too much power over you? Has it left you vulnerable to hurts within the church or organized religion? How has it affected the way you view God?

CHAPTER 3

RELIGION MADE WHOLE

Every human being was created by God primarily to know Him,
love Him, and serve Him. All other activity is superfluous.

GEORGE BARNA, *REVOLUTION*

SAY THE WORD *RELIGION* and watch people bristle.
There's just something about it that causes resistance,
and not just among nonbelievers—Jesus-following
people who don't want to be associated with things that
seem cold or contrived don't like it either. What we
really want is spiritual vibrancy of a lasting kind, and we
have become increasingly skeptical that religion can fit in
that space. Religion itself is not to blame; our religious
attempt to impress others or make ourselves feel close
to God is responsible. But as a person who has lived the
experiences of both playing church and having a new

life of spiritual vibrancy, I do not find it contradictory that I consider myself to be in spiritual recovery, and yet I passionately love the church. Both states are possible, no matter how much at odds they may seem to be.

Recovery

The recovery part is easy—in theory, at least. I spent years feeding my addiction to religion through my spiritual performance. But by the time I was nearly through my first two years of college, most of my spiritual decorations had already been pretty well stripped away by virtue of my own rebellion. The more frequent and intense my partying became, the harder it became to play the role and keep up the good-pastor's-daughter image. Still, there was a piece of me that held on to that old addiction. The part that couldn't bear the thought of being found out as a fraud kept me coming back, ironically, to the safe haven of inauthenticity. I kept my own best secret. But inside, my heart screamed in rebellion against what wasn't real. It was killing me on the inside and creating a deep, secret hole, much like the anguish the psalmist David described (in his case, when he acknowledged his unconfessed sin), "I was weak and miserable, and I groaned all day long" (Psalm 32:3).

I was so disillusioned by my own inauthenticity at that point—so hungry for something real—that I began to seek Him through more primitive measures. The only way I knew how to make sense of the Jesus world in which I was so intensely ingrained was to go back and revisit what I had learned about God as a child. I began to grapple with questions that dug into the very core of my faith. *Have I believed in a fraud all these years? Or is it just that I am one, myself?* Over time, my eyes opened to the answer.

Enter my recovery. As my primitive search for Jesus continued, I began opening the Word and reading it for myself. My church tradition had fed regular doses of Scripture to me—which, without my own hunt for its spiritual food, was enough to keep me feeling religious through the week but not enough to power a real, personal knowledge of God. Fear ensured that my efforts would be silent and solo, for a time threatening to use my own attempts to shame me. *Pastors' daughters are supposed to know what the Bible says*, I chided myself, warning, *No one can ever find out how much I don't know.* But even as I was motivated to keep my infantile knowledge of the Word private, unable to handle outside judgment, I was becoming increasingly open with the only One who knew of my hypocrisy. Somehow, I knew I could still trust Him . . . and that trust bonded us. Quietly, unassumingly, my holes were driving me to Him.

It's true that part of the initial motivation for private

Bible study was the fact that I didn't know what else to do to help myself that no one would have to know about. I had tried the feigning-knowledge route, and it didn't get me any closer to feeling something real between God and me, something I couldn't live without. Looking back now, I see the benefit—a desperate break with our former way of living is often the best first step we can take. The other motivating factor was that I still held on to the hope that reading the Bible might somehow actually change my life. For a while, commitment alone kept me going, especially on the days I did not learn something I considered revolutionary. But over time, the power of the Word became more clear and real to me. I began to see God in a different light. I found Him to be more powerful than I remembered. I started to feel honored that He would love me. The act of reading the Word without a set formula or dependence on another to teach it to me slowly but steadily made me feel different, less defined by a ritual. I was starting to believe that maybe what my church schooling had taught me for years was really true: that I would know God when I read His Word.

That is the beauty of being in spiritual recovery. It is what happens when we choose the thing that will make our soul well, even without the specific understanding of all its many benefits. When we are no longer weighed down by the expectations of a misplaced faith in religion for its own sake, we are free to develop the personal communion with God we were created to enjoy (see 1 Corinthians 1:9). That doesn't mean our spiritual life will be perfect. Now, years removed from that first difficult "detox," my addiction to religiosity still sometimes woos me. But though it threatens to disrupt my connection with God, the relationship forged from my recovery allows me to be able to resist it. I've been in that place. I don't want to go back.

Remembering what it felt like before God filled the religious hole is vital because it helps us become desperate to keep moving forward. Though the Word tells us we are ultimate overcomers through Christ (Romans 8:37) and I believe this, I also believe that the management of our life on a daily basis is what keeps us from sinking into a deep pit we must climb out of. Dying to self daily, as taught in Luke 9:23, is a practice that includes laying down even those religious things that we have come to depend upon that have kept us from a clear mind and heart for God. A large part of that is being aware of the risk of religious addiction and allowing our Father to help us live an abundant life of recovery. This type of spiritual recovery is the very essence of what wholeness in our religion means to our life: What was once closed is now open. What was once feigned is now genuine. What was once rigid is now tender and yielding. The thriving, limitless life of a true spiritual journey with Jesus is what has kept me, many times over, from caving to the temptation to adorn myself with fancy, empty Jesus wear.

I know, and you may know, too, that the most desperate place to be is the one where you cannot feel God. It is eerie and still there, cold and stale. It is painful in a way that nothing quite compares to, a place of nothingness that drives us to become desperate enough to ask Him to move in any way He chooses, even if it's radical, just so we can feel Him. It is the glorious start of every hole-filled religious addict's recovery: we desire to fully experience God.

A sober consequence of having lived inconsistently or being outed (even by yourself, as I was) as a spiritual fraud is that when we begin to talk about Jesus again, some may be skeptical. It can be intimidating to realize that people may not believe that this aspect of our life is now very real, a possibility that may even threaten to stifle us. But we can't let that deter us from sharing about our spiritual journey. The truth is, some critics will never be convinced. But skepticism brings great opportunity to display the transformative work of Jesus in our life, and our holes are the first half of that metamorphosis. When things look different, Jesus can be seen as the great change agent He is, the One who filled our holes to create wholeness, and we become His powerful visual aid. We will relate to Paul, former persecutor of the faithful, in his joy over people seeing for themselves the way Jesus Christ changed his life: "People were saying, 'The one who used to persecute us is now preaching the very faith he tried to destroy!' And they praised God because of me" (Galatians 1:23-24). I can think of no more palpable testimony. I can find no greater purpose than to be used by God to tell that holes-to-wholeness story by the proof of a changed life.

Through those years I wore a hole from my religion, I often felt like I was swimming in a bottomless, boundless pool of deep, black lake water, just seconds before slipping underneath its surface, never to be seen again. As I peer inside the window of my wholeness now, I see myself being thrown a buoy, just in time, having just enough strength to grab on and allow myself to be rescued. It drives my resolve to answer any lingering outside skepticism—even from myself—because I have been rescued from a life of spiritual inauthenticity that felt like a death sentence. God saved me from myself, and I couldn't be more grateful. Spiritual recovery means that I'll never get over the fact that I was once drowning in the bottomless pit of my religion, but He never would let me slip forever away.

I was saved once, but in my process of finding what was real, twice He made me whole.

Loving the Church

How I came to love the church is a bit more complicated, and that is an important part of the journey as well. Where I come from, it's almost a sin to even say you might not love the church. But for a time in my life, I didn't.

I had my reasons, and many of them were valid. My family had been hurt by handfuls of church people through the years of ministry, some of them small wounds compared to what would come, but almost innately I knew at an early age that not everyone who sat in the pews could be trusted. So I didn't. My parents never fostered this in me, and in contrast, did an amazing job of attempting to keep me grounded and open to the loving arms of caring church people. But I had eyes and ears. I was more perceptive than people may have thought, and I was listening when they thought I wasn't. The dad I knew at home was my hero. The pastor-dad I knew on stage was important and beloved, but controversial. It was hard for me to reconcile, and there were times that the noise of disgruntled church people grew very loud inside my young ears.

The irony here is that we in the church were meant to be loud, but in a different way. Jesus created us to be salt and light (Matthew 5:13-14) and to spread His message of love and grace and peace. Where there is spiritual blandness, we are to provide savor. Where there is spiritual darkness, we are to provide illumination. We are to draw people to Jesus by our loud display of His abundant love. Unfortunately, we often use our voices in a way that doesn't represent Him as He really is, thereby forfeiting our ability to show anyone His real worth.

But there is good news. What wholeness in our religion brings us is rich: we win back our ability to influence. Where our holes once limited us, our whole-ness will now propel us into becoming the believers we were always meant to be. We will begin to see the beauty in the undoing of what once defined us and drove us to reject people in the process. Instead of being some-thing we are reluctant to associate with, the church will become a place of healing and hope as it was intended. It is the reason this holes-to-wholeness process is so vital—because in order for the church to buoy its influence and effectively reach souls, we must first be spiritually well. Wholeness in our religion allows us to do that.

At this point in my life, my experience with the church ministry business threatened to derail my trust in Jesus—a place familiar to many people I have met in years since. Reaching a place of understanding and love for the church and Jesus was made possible by the choice I had made before and would make again: to seek the things that would lead to wholeness, making my soul well. This is the catalytic choice of every person who has had a difficulty with the church or a religious disillusionment—a choice that can determine the course of a spiritual future. Emerging from such disappointments whole requires choosing the path of dedicated prayer, reading of the Word, and a strong resistance

What wholeness in our religion brings us is rich: we win back our ability to influence.

to the defining or limiting influence of difficulty. It is the way I reconcile the coexistence of being in spiritual recovery—detoxing from ritual and formulas to know God—while still believing in and loving the church.

But loving the church does not always come easy. The natural response when we have been let down by the church is to close ourselves off from other believers or even from God—self-protection that seems easier. But left to fester, the loss of community and disillusionment can leave a deep hole in our religion. We are vulnerable at this point and susceptible to developing more holes if we do not maintain constant fellowship with God. It was just such a pivotal moment in my early twenties— in response to the circumstances threatening to pull me back to an unhealthy spiritual place—that landed me on the crisp white couch of a counselor in my first true experience with therapy.

Dr. Curt looked intimidating, to say the least, and a part of me wanted to run out the door the minute I sat down. I probably would have, had I been able to come up with a viable excuse. But I stayed put, and he began to ask questions. What brought me in today? What did I want to talk about? How could he help me?

I didn't feel like answering his questions. In fact, they suddenly set off a volcano inside. *How do I know how you can help me, professional doctor-man?* Except in my heart, I screamed an expletive—which was significant for a clean-mouthed girl like me. I had reached the breaking point and couldn't take the formalities anymore. *I'm just here because my dad screwed up, some church people screwed him over, and I'm the roadkill left behind!*

I heard my voice say something different, more civilized; words that held together my crumbling resilience. Slowly, methodically, accurately, I detailed the church story that had literally changed my life. But in the midst of my factual account, I heard myself saying something so honest it scared me: "I love my dad, and I love the church, but I hate at least one of them. Now tell me what to do with that!"

As the words flowed out of me, so did the tears.

What I had most feared admitting to myself, I had just admitted out loud. Now I could only wonder whether I had become one of those Christians who rejected people because of their flawed humanity—my father, the church—the same thing I now despised about church people who had hurt my family and me. Would my own judgmental attitude cause a Christian shrink I didn't know to send me away carelessly, like I felt the church had?

Dr. Curt didn't flinch. He didn't come over and embrace my now sobbing, despair-wrenched body, as part of me wanted him to. Instead, he did something better. From his chair and with a steady gaze that ran right through me, he spoke over me these profound, life-changing words: "Both of them made mistakes. Let them be human, and let your love for them be enough to extinguish the hate."

Truly, these words changed my life. Even now, they ring in my ears when I am disappointed by church leadership, believers, and even myself. Love can prevail over even our deepest of hurts, as Proverbs 10:12 says: "Love covers over all wrongs" (NIV). We have to allow for humanness—yes, even our own—while believing in a love bigger than ourselves with the ability to cover all. If Jesus could love amidst a crowd full of angry haters who wanted Him dead, can we not allow for the fleshly mistakes and grievances of others?

Grace. It is difficult. But where holes from our religion limit it, wholeness allows it to be possible. For us to truly be able to love the church, grace has to prevail. When it does, our capacity to love and minister will expand in extraordinary ways—reaching to our family, other people, and ourselves. This is what Dr. Curt was talking about, and it would only be realized if I chose to let God fill up my holes from the church and make me whole. Loving my dad through his mistakes was far easier for me, as the bond we have cannot be undone, and I recall the grace he has always given to me. But loving the church was more challenging, yet it was the more pivotal decision because it would require a deeper filling of Jesus. Often, the things we find most demanding and difficult are the very places we most need to have healed.

I resist spending a lot of time explaining why church people sometimes behave poorly, mainly because it's not all that productive. It is what it is and will always be, until the day we are all perfected and made new by our heavenly reunion with Christ—the day we become truly and fully whole. While we are here on earth, the tendency toward hypocrisy lives within all of us. Our wholeness allows us to be spiritually messy yet make peace with the church, with Jesus being the healing agent behind both.

Spiritual Vibrancy

The presence of God—not how well we can perform duties of religion—is what creates within us a spiritual vibrancy. This distinction is referenced by Paul: "They will act as if they are religious, but they will reject the power that could make them godly" (2 Timothy 3:5). Vibrancy doesn't come to us through our religious efforts, although discipline, growth, and knowledge may. But vibrancy— life within our soul—is the effective work of Jesus.

We can't pretend our way into a powerful prayer life. Knowledge won't give us impact. We won't authentically display something we don't feel from within. It's not that we should discount religion; it's that we should recognize it as being less important than Jesus. The presence of God in our life will produce a thriving spiritual existence that nothing else can generate—creating a genuine passion and concern for those things that once did not compel us.

It's a metamorphosis I have watched develop in my own life. Out of all the ugly things I have ever admitted out loud, the acknowledgment of being apathetic to people and things around me has been the hardest, as if in my admission, I confess to not having a soul. Who is cold enough to say they just don't care? Who is honest enough to admit something so blatantly at odds with the gospel? Like other believers who allow the gospel to become largely self-serving, I was most concerned with things that directly benefited me and focused on those aspects, things like the ability of God to help me through tough times and the promises of His faith-ful love. When religion was primary, those things served me well. It never asked me to go beyond and reach further.

The presence of God—not how well we can perform duties of religion—is what creates within us a spiritual vibrancy.

My holes had narrowed my spiritual vision so much that I was not able to see God's bigger picture. Care about widows and orphans? Not really. Think about poverty? Not much. Desire to evangelize? Only if the opportunity fell into my lap in a moment I felt really spiritual. This is where shame is born in many believers who carry these same private thoughts, but we are too ashamed to admit them, even to ourselves. It is a help-less, empty feeling to know that we do not have the depth required to care for these things, only to try to manufacture those feelings on our own and watch ourselves fall short. This happens because our flesh does not naturally crave service or selflessness. Instead, it desires things that directly benefit us: "I know that nothing good lives in me, that is, in my sinful nature" (Romans 7:18).

But when we become whole in our religion, the gospel becomes far less about what we can gain and much more about what we can give. We become inspired by the life of Jesus Christ, and we want to emulate His extravagant love. Our hearts break over what breaks His. Our spirits become fully alive and our spiritual senses awaken. A natural and deep care develops, sensitizing our soul . . . compelling our actions. When that happens, we will know that our religion has been made whole. Simply put, we feel differently about things and it flows out of us. Our service becomes grittier, getting our hands dirtier as we become more radical in our faith. We care about all aspects of the gospel.

Something else that happens when our religion is made whole is that we develop a solid faith that's less susceptible to the shifting tides of worldly beliefs. It is the principle I mentioned from Matthew 7, of the house built on the solid foundation of Jesus rather than the variable sands of religion. Our deep spiritual connection grounds us with Jesus, and there's nothing more we need in this day to see us through.

I can admit that there have been moments in my life when I have wished for a way in the back door— a way that satisfies my need for the easy and concrete.

If I can only learn one more formula, maybe that will be it. If I can only read one more book, maybe it will unlock that one elusive truth that will change my life. If I go to just one more Bible study or attend one more worship experience, maybe it will connect me to God. The truth is, it never will. While we depend on those things to make us spiritual, God seeks our dependence upon Him to make us whole.

The outpouring of Jesus from our life that happens when we become spiritually vibrant is sweeping. We watch Him use us in ways our religious rigors would never have made possible, which gives us a taste of what being a representative of Jesus really means, and in turn, we crave to be used by God again. I believe this is one of the core reasons Jesus made the distinction between religion and godliness in Matthew 7:21: "Not everyone who calls out to me, 'Lord! Lord!' will enter the Kingdom of Heaven. Only those who actually do the will of my Father in heaven will enter." He knew that though we would be drawn toward religion, our influence would be found in godliness. Having lived many years with a manufactured faith manifested in rules and rituals but without real depth, I now know that nothing could feel more fulfilling. This is how I felt when a few years ago I became reconnected to a guy named Chad.

Represent Him Well

There are some people who never leave your mind, no matter the span of time. Chad is one of those people for me—a guy I went to high school with back in the days of big hair, big eighties music, and (my) big attitude. It may be the reason Chad and I hit it off right from the start. He was as big and bold as I, though in a bit of a different way. Our sarcasm ran in tandem, and he made me laugh every day.

So when he requested my friendship on Facebook some twenty years later, I couldn't have been more thrilled. I didn't know where the years had taken him, but I was pretty sure it wouldn't matter. We shared the bond of attending a small Christian school together, and we had been the kind of friends who would always relate.

Several weeks and an e-mail to my in-box later, I realized how wrong I was. Chad wrote to inform me that he was going to need to sever our newly formed Facebook friendship, as I was annoying him with all my Jesus talk. Surprised and disappointed, I understood a bit more of his reasoning as I continued reading. He shared with me a few things about his twenty-year journey and that the religious faith he had once professed, he now denounced. Over the years since I'd seen him, he'd become agnostic.

But that wasn't quite all. He said some hard things

to me—hard things to hear, to sort through, to be willing to look at closely. He doubted I was sincere. He questioned my authenticity. He told me that the Lisa he knew back in high school was bold and fearless, and the one he was hearing now was simply just a follower—a less-than-real writer who used overspiritualized analogies to relate to God. I wanted to hide my face from its sting. His words mercilessly tap-danced on every insecurity I had, every place of guilt over my past spiritual addiction, plunging way down deep into the darkest place of my recovery—a place where, given permission, another dark hole could be fostered. His words hurt. The possibility they might be true hurt even worse.

After pulling my chin off the ground, I let his vitriol sink in. A fake. A fraud. A phony. Was I those things anymore? It wasn't that much of a stretch. Ironically, the Lisa he had known before was all those things then, but he couldn't have known that because we didn't have any real conversations about God that I could ever remember. It made me sad to think that the real, authentic Lisa, who had changed significantly since those days, was someone he never got a chance to know—she wasn't around during those years of study hall. I was finally at a place in my life now where inauthenticity felt worse than the honest truth, though part of me fought the temptation to choose poorly: to run and hide from Chad's accusations or maybe even worse—offer some type of shiny, saintly manifesto.

Reluctantly, I took to my knees. I knew I needed to talk to God and ask Him to put my heart in the spotlight. I feared hearing from Him lest He speak insights that hurt, yet I feared not hearing from Him even more. Was this the one time He wouldn't be there? Was He too disappointed by my actions in the past that He was finally wiping His hands clean of me? I braced myself for what might be an excruciatingly painful moment on His anvil of truth, prepared to be shown the weak places He might need to forge stronger.

In a quiet voice I spoke these words aloud. I was grateful that in the moment, only my sweet little dog, sitting faithfully at my feet, and Jesus would hear them.

"Is this true, God?" I asked. "Is what Chad is saying about me true? Am I the person he thinks I am? Because if I am, we have a lot more work to do."

It was only a matter of seconds before graciously, specifically, He spoke to my heart. It was as if He knew His silence in this space was not what I most needed. But His response was not exactly what I expected. Instead of answering me directly, He challenged me with a request.

Represent Me well, Lisa. Just represent Me well.

Random thoughts came flooding into my brain: pictures of unknown faces of church people who didn't represent Jesus well to my friend Chad and what they might have done and said. Flashes of me through the years with all my outward, shiny spiritual decorations. Fake-outs, cop-outs . . . and the Jesus talk that sounded good but made me want to vomit. And finally, the choices I'd made to change my life and how those holes of my religion didn't define me any longer. Instantly, the wholeness of my Jesus overwhelmed me as I rested in the words I felt Him speaking over me.

You aren't who you used to be, Lisa. You have been changed. You have the power inside you to represent the One who has healed your inauthenticity and made you whole. You are able to do this well.

I wept in gratitude, still unable to fully comprehend the ways that Jesus had changed my life. But I knew that my life would no longer be about getting someone to like me or understand the depths of my passion for Jesus. I knew that the hole of my religion had been filled through the gentle guiding influence of God, and that my life mantra had now become: *like me or not, I just pray that you cannot deny the presence of God in my life.* At the end of the day, that is what would draw Chad and others like him to Jesus, and I could safely rest in it.

As I write this today, I don't know what your life mantra is or where your spiritual journey has taken you so far. You may be heavily in the throes of spiritual recovery or on a wellness journey that is helping you learn how to truly love the church. Maybe you desire to care about the entire gospel or you want to build your life on a faith that is solid. These things, as with the power to represent Jesus well, are only possible through a religion made whole. To know that you have been a part of showing someone the great benefits of God is a place your addiction to spiritual things will never take you—a place that helps strengthen your faith in the power of the presence of God. It bolsters your desire to stay present in a place of spiritual vibrancy, where holes are not allowed to develop into limiting factors in your spiritual life. It makes your commitment to authenticity worth it, even in those moments when you are faced with the choice of seeing your own hard truth. This is a promise, my friend, I can passionately make. It is the promise of wholeness.

There is no shortcut to becoming an accurate representative of a beautiful, loving God. At the same time, it is not a complicated process—it's so simple, in fact, that people often overlook it. The key to being real is *readying your heart for the outflow of His Spirit*. That means getting into the Word and reading it for yourself. It means dedicated, honest, earnest prayer that aggressively pursues knowing God. It means a commitment to focusing on what is real, pursuing spiritual recovery, desiring the vibrancy of God, and positioning yourself to represent Him well. The by-product of those things is you, made whole, and your beautiful ability to influence others by your life. There is no higher calling or greater fulfillment.

You may be wondering about the end of the Chad story. Thankfully, there is no end in sight, as our friendship door remains mutually open. After sitting on it for a few days, I answered his e-mail with another. He didn't respond immediately, but he didn't end our Facebook relationship either. In my message, I told him I was still very much the same bold, outspoken girl he knew in high school. Only now I was speaking out for the things that had substance, from a heart that did too. I told him I understood if he wanted to sever ties with me, but I wished he wouldn't. I told him about how Jesus changed my life and how that drove my passion. I told him I had considered his thoughts and could only continue to pray that they were not true.

And then I thanked Jesus that His wholeness could make a religious addict recover . . . an embittered girl feel merciful . . . and an inauthentic soul become spiritually complete. All of this, and so much more, is what He stands ready to do for us all when we choose to be made well.

Questions to Consider

1. How can the hole of our religion actually benefit us? How does it drive us to God, and what do we seek from Him?

2. What does it mean to you to be spiritually vibrant? How does wholeness make that possible?

CHAPTER 4

THE HOLE OF ROLES

If you board the wrong train,
it is no use running along the corridor in the opposite direction.

DIETRICH BONHOEFFER

DEEP IN THE HEART OF THE MIDWEST, just a year after
the dramatic scandals of televangelists Jim Bakker and
Jimmy Swaggart, another preacher named Jim stood to
lose everything.

He had built his mega-church ministry in a bit of a
different way than those who bore a brighter spotlight,
but with a similar determination. A rugged cowboy
at heart, Jim never really knew his limits. His mother
often told the story of the time her rowdy young son ran
into the living room shooting toy guns in each hand,
announcing, "I'm a cowboy preacher! I'm gonna preach

to people and tell them about Jesus." Even then, both his intense love for the great outdoors and his passion to share the message of Christ with his unique style were unmistakable.

For thirty years, that is exactly what cowboy preacher Jim did. But a few years before, young wannabe cowboy preacher Jim got off track. As he grew, the foolishness and recklessness of youth overshadowed his preaching dreams and he wandered away from God, eventually finding himself on an enormous US Navy ship with a fresh, colorful arm tattoo that said, *Mi Vida Torcida*— "My Twisted Life." His arm told a true story: adrift from Jesus, his world had become twisted indeed.

He came off the boat at age twenty-one to a welcoming family but with a heart full of emptiness. He knew the things of the world had not satisfied, partly because he had tried them and partly because the relentless call of Jesus, though quieter, had never completely gone away. Even on the big ship, God was drawing Jim to Himself.

Unbeknownst to Jim, throughout the years of his running, his mother was praying long and hard that like the proverbial Prodigal Son, he would one day find himself back in a place of spiritual surrender. It seemed that her prayers were working.

One night shortly after Jim came home, he was sitting

in his room, surrounded by the silence of his solitude. His thoughts were about his life and how, up to this point, he'd tried everything in the world but God. With brutal honesty, he looked up to the white ceiling and spoke these words: "God, if You're there, I'm gonna try You." It was at that moment of simple, heartfelt pursuit that Jesus drew near, and Jim's heart became pliable.

The next day, Jim asked his mother if he could see her preacher. While he had been out sailing the seas, Jim's family had moved to a different state and found a local Baptist church they enjoyed attending, pastored by a man named John. John was a real "man's man," a former football player, the kind of guy a rugged outdoorsman like Jim could appreciate. Thrilled by the spiritual movement she was seeing, Jim's mother immediately arranged a meeting between Jim and Pastor John for later that day.

On the way out the door to meet John, Jim grabbed the first Bible he saw, naive to any type of religious protocol: a big, hard-backed family Bible with printed pictures and bold black print. He tucked it awkwardly under his muscled arm, where it stayed for the entire car ride as he cried all the way to the church. Pursuing Jesus at this moment was just one of the many times his steely determination and budding faith in God would prove to be one of the greatest gifts of his life.

Pastor John welcomed Jim into the church, praying with him—leading him to know Christ in a more intimate way. They formed a lasting bond that day—a divine connection that proved significant through the years. After that, Jim's life was never the same. He enrolled in Bible college within months. The mighty hand of God had stoked the fire and passion that burned within him, and he was driven to make good on his childhood promise to become that audacious cowboy preacher.

When he started school that fall, unaware of many of the social graces he had missed learning while sailing the seas, it was obvious to those who met him that the world had been his teacher. His strong confidence powered him forward, and his raw charisma and movie-star good looks endeared him to people—in particular, to a beautiful young woman named Kathie.

Kathie was everything Jim wasn't: conventional, soft, and wholesome. The purity of Kathie's life intrigued Jim on every level. She was raised by conservative, godly parents. She was Homecoming Queen. She was the most angelic thing Jim had ever seen and the kindest person he had ever known—so incredible, as he tells it, that he almost didn't know what to do with her but make her his wife. For her part, Kathie was enamored with Jim's strength and maturity, and she shared his desire to live a life of ministry. After a whirlwind three-month

courtship and a six-month engagement, Kathie and Jim
were married.

From day one, their life together became that of an
exciting spiritual pilgrimage. They did not know what
lay ahead (maybe for the better); all they knew was
that they wanted to serve God together. Jim's gift of
communicating the gospel afforded him multiple opportunities for pastorates right away. He dove deep into the
Bible and saturated himself in its words like a sponge,
wringing out its truth for the sermon every Sunday. He
couldn't have hidden his deep passion for Jesus if he'd
tried. It was what drove him, for years and in multiple
congregations, right up until the time he found himself
standing in front of a church he dearly loved, resigning
on a warm Sunday night in a cloud of shame and suspicion over the actions that forced him out of his pulpit.

I remember that day in 1994 well. It was the day my
dad, cowboy Jim, and I lost our roles.

Hinge Moments of Change

One of the most curious things about humans is how
hard we resist change. Even when our lives unravel
before us, there is still something inside that holds on to
the mess just so we don't have to do something different.
Though we may cry out for a reprieve from our holes
when faced with their effects, when we start to change

for the better, suddenly we long for their comfortable familiarity. The loss of a role we love or have identified ourselves with is no different. In the moments we most cling to the roles that have defined us, we fail to realize that losing what we think we are opens up the opportunity for God to show us our true created self.

What happened with my dad in his role as pastor of a church affected not just him or his ministry. In most such moments in life, the ramifications of what happens next aren't usually relegated to those it will directly touch. Often it causes a ripple—both far-reaching and widespread, largely determined by the path we choose. Certainly, this was our family's experience, by way of a decision by church leadership to let him go. The loss of my father's role in the church affected the entire family—the least of which was our living situation, his loss of income, and the embarrassment of seeing the story splashed on the front page of the local paper and on the nightly news. In fact, the difficulty of being on the receiving end of gossip and insinuation paled in comparison to the pain of being a bystander to something that hurt so many people.

At this point it's important for you to understand how tightly the threads between my father and me are really tied. He was the first man to ever have my heart, and I loved him in a way that only a daughter really knows. After five years of unsuccessful attempts to have a child, my parents had been thrilled to welcome their firstborn child, a son, and I came eighteen months later; my sister, nearly twelve long years after that. All of us grew up feeling deeply wanted, cherished, and protected. But my father and I have always been close.

He was always larger than life to me. I couldn't have been older than five when I remember staring at him in church and thinking he was the best-looking man I had ever seen. With the swagger of Elvis and the rugged, country-boy appeal of the Marlboro Man, he owned every room he walked into. Every stage he graced, he commanded. He had a drive and a focus that could not be denied. As the years went by, though, those two traits would prove to make him both beloved and disliked—a polarizing paradox for a mega-church pastor, but one that often characterizes a leader.

In all his years of pastoring, he had not forgotten his love of the great outdoors—hunting, in particular. My mother had the enormous task of making the wall-to-wall deer heads adorning our living room look festive every Christmas, and somehow she managed. My brother and I got used to seeing Dad disappear into the woods in early fall of every year, eager to spend cold mornings painted up in a deer stand in the Middle of Nowhere, USA. Skinned deer carcasses hung by their skinny legs in our garage, and game nights at our house meant you brought over what you killed and my mom would cook it up in her Crock-Pot. I can still remember eating moose for the very first time and spitting it out when my mom told me what it was.

It came as little surprise to us when my father's hobby of hunting turned into collecting deer antlers, and his hobby of collecting deer antlers turned into a full-blown business of buying and selling them. It was a natural progression, really, as things that were in my dad's hands never stayed small for long. With his personality, he was primed and ready for success in anything that had his attention. In his church position, he was a visionary and a leader who ran on constant overdrive; he simply applied those characteristics to his additional role of deer-antler broker. Great at discovering cast-off sheds (horns that have been shed for new ones) and old farmers' cobweb-collecting, diamond-in-the-rough finds, Dad soon became the darling of this very rustic type of art collecting.

Juggling the incredible business his simple hobby had turned out to be fueled his need for challenge but compromised his role at the church—and it didn't take long for people to notice. Within months, he watched his hobby-turned-business result in six-figure profits, as his world soon filled with high-paying collectors, waving money in his face and enticing him with the unspoken promise of paying for his family's growing needs. With his dream of one day having a traveling sportsman ministry full of deer heads to display, it seemed like a step in the right direction, especially since none of his actions were illegal. But they were, at the very least, distracting—pushing him to the edge of his commitments. His already-busy days became even more frantic. More times than I can count, dinners at home with him consisted of him holding the phone between his shoulder and his chin, writing things that looked like numbers down on a white dinner napkin. Little did any of us know at the time how important those napkin scrawlings would be.

About a year into his new business venture, in this napkin-writing heyday, I came home from a friend's house on a sunny Saturday afternoon to discover a car I didn't recognize in our driveway. I smiled to myself, sure that a member of the congregation had dropped something by in a random act of kindness, something I had grown accustomed to. From the driveway to the front door, I played my own little mind game of Who Might It Be.

When I opened the front door I saw not my favorite deacon or the pianist bringing flowers—but the whiteness of my mom's face. It was a look unlike any I had ever seen before, because rarely did things ever rattle her. And that immediately rattled me. I felt a vice grip of fear in my teenage chest like I had never before known, as if I knew innately that this moment was one that would forever change my life. I didn't know the specifics, but what I did know was that my dad was home in the middle of a day he was usually at his office, studying, and he was sitting at our kitchen table with a man I didn't know and who was dressed in all khaki, two things that were very much out of the ordinary.

"Go down to your room, Lisa," my father spoke, deep and firm. His tone was different—tense. I knew that if he hadn't been burdened by something, he would have greeted me with a smile and a "welcome home." I could see only his profile—the dark outline of his face and hair. Even more troubling was the man in khaki. Despite the tone of command in my dad's voice, which usually stirred any audience, the man never moved.

I went down to my room that day and tried to do something normal, though somewhere within I knew my world could become very different. It was a "hinge moment" in my life, not unlike what you may know. It is that moment when you find yourself at a place where life has taken a new direction without your permission. It is what happens when the undercurrent of a changing role is lapping at your feet and you are resisting the idea that it might carry you away. It is the place where, historically, many holes like mine have been made.

The Aftermath

None of us knew—certainly not I—what the visit from the man in khaki would do to change my family's life. All I can tell you is that sometimes life hits you like a tsunami on crack: where everything you thought you knew about your life is wrecked, all because of something you couldn't stop.

A tsunami on crack. I can find no better way to describe the irrational way life can rip us away from our roles and leave us dangling in the wake of such a separation. I can remember hearing eyewitness accounts from the massive Indian Ocean tsunami of 2004. Many of the victims shared the same recollections: survivors clinging to large pieces of debris . . . cries, screams, and desperate pleas for help . . . determined victims separated from those they loved, trying to preserve life as they knew it. These survivors endured something much greater than the loss of a role—they fought to save their very lives. But the parallel of surviving the separation of a role we want to hang on to is that it challenges everything we think we are when it is taken away. Especially when that role has been tied to our life's identity.

The news that fateful day at my house delivered by

the man in khaki would, in every sense of the word, rock my family to its core. Eventually, it would unwittingly separate us all from the roles we had grown to know and love, especially my father, cowboy preacher Jim. The man in khaki was a federal agent, having come to inform him that in one of his recent deer-head brokering transactions, he had broken a federal law by crossing over state lines with a deer head he had neglected to purchase a two-dollar permit for. It was a law both my father and the old farmer who had sold him the head were unaware of, but that didn't matter. The law had been broken, and now my father was in trouble.

The depth of the trouble we didn't at first know. It seemed, for a short time, as if things were going to be okay and my always-capable father would be able to maneuver out of this costly mistake by managing the crazy mess and straightening it all out. Still, as a questioner, I wanted to know exactly what was going on. My questions started that first night after the man in khaki left. After my relentless probing, my mother finally told me a few sketchy details (all she knew at the time) about what would eventually turn into my family's very real nightmare: my dad had unknowingly broken a law, plain and simple. That was about all she could tell me. In the way only mothers can, she made me feel safe and taken care of, reassuring me enough to sleep that night and many nights after. But even while I slept, the tsunami rumbled.

In a way, it is something we learned to live with, as many people do when faced with an ongoing entangle-ment. Over time it became our new normal to live with the dysfunction of my father's endurance of federal investigations, phone calls with lawyers, threats of jail time, and high levels of suspicion and insinuation. There were moments of reprieve—no more than a few weeks at a time, but we welcomed them anyway. The small victo-ries we experienced were moments we were able to come up for air from the suffocation of the big waves that continued to threaten our well-being.

In the five years that the investigations went on, there were lots of twists and turns and more than a few scary moments. When it was just (and by *just*, I mean no one else investigating him at the time) the federal fish and game commission that was doing the investigating, Dad was hanging on with a fairly strong grip. But even so, he was dealing with things he had no experience with, like looking in the rearview mirror of his truck as he drove through town and realizing he was being followed. This happened on more than one occasion, and it created a sense of paranoia in him. This only exacerbated the level of suspicion some people already had that he was doing things he shouldn't have been, as the paranoia caused him to act even more frenetic. All the time he was managing his business mess, he was putting on his suit, going into the office of the church, and trying to be a pastor.

After several years, the federal fish and game commission couldn't find enough evidence to make charges stick, so they turned things over to the IRS, the one place that was eager to try. It was perfect timing for a storm of new allegations leveled Dad's way, as the feeding frenzy of high-profile pastors' scandals was already well into its heyday. I can remember like it was yesterday several experiences during that time, like the one when we were on a family vacation in Florida and my father received a phone call in the hotel room from his frightened secretary, saying that federal agents were in his office at that very moment, raiding it. As always, he tried to shelter me from whatever in life looked scary. All I knew was that it seemed a lot like TV. Bad people got their offices raided—people who had done wrong things. Convicts. Certainly not people like my Jesus-loving father.

As you can imagine, the journey from days like that to the final day of reckoning was long. In the end, after years of whispers, maneuverings, threats, and tears, my father's ministry could no longer be preserved. The days of his poor napkin-scrawled record keeping had caught up with him, and he was presented with two options by an eager prosecutor: either he could plead guilty on two years of underreporting income and pay a fine or else be indicted on six years of tax evasion and spend the next several months in an expensive trial whose outcome was unclear. To save all involved parties from this trial, he chose to plead guilty and was swiftly indicted in court for understating his taxes for several years.

The image of my parents walking into court, splashed on front-page news, was one no church wants for its pastor. A few weeks prior to Dad's day in court, the leadership of the church had decided they did not want to continue to follow a man with a tarnished reputation, and as a result, they asked him to resign.

I don't hold judgment for this decision. It was a tough position to be in, for everyone. But what I can say from my own experience is that watching my dad resign from his beloved church, from a pulpit that had been his for thirteen years, nearly shattered my heart. I knew that although his business activities had led to this moment, being forced to leave a role he so deeply loved would be excruciating. And it would create a hole the size of a crater in me—one I wasn't sure could ever be filled.

Giving Permission

After reading so much of my father's story, I hope you won't forget about your own. We have all had (or will have) roles that consume the way we view our life purpose and may be taken from us without our permission. Both can be defining: those roles we have grown accustomed to and currently embody, and the ones we have had painfully stripped away. My friend Miles, who once worked as a corporate executive and now sweeps the floors of a school cafeteria to earn money to keep the heat on in his house, never told the company who fired him that he was willing to let go of his role there. My former neighbor Christine never gave permission to the semi that ran head-on into her husband and took away her role as his wife when the crash killed him instantly. The roles we have in life often hold our hearts in their hands, so when the roles are taken away, our hearts are dropped and broken. We have depended on them to fulfill us, and that has created a hole.

The truth is, our roles *should* matter to us. They should be important and we should nurture them, value them, and love them. I'll never get over the gift of getting to be a wife to my husband and a mom to my kids. I'll never stop appreciating what it feels like to be someone's daughter, granddaughter, sister, cousin, and friend. The gift of wearing the role of author/communicator of words that help lead people to the feet of Jesus is humbling, extravagant, overwhelming. But these roles do not make me who I am at the very core. They are simply what I am blessed to do while God chooses to leave me here on earth.

Sometimes the length of time we get to wear these roles we love is not to our liking. We have expectations for the roles that we have been blessed with, and often that does not include their loss. So it makes sense that we grasp the things that have become important parts of our identity and hang on to them for our very life, refusing the idea that they are allowed to separate from us.

But—and there is a *but*—even though in our human condition it is understandable that we cling to these roles, doing so is often the very thing that leads to the loss of ourselves. It reminds me of the old story about the monkey who wanted so much he wound up losing it all. He was stealing food in his town until one day a juggler visited and determined to rid the town of his nuisances. He asked for some jars with narrow necks, placed peanuts in them, and put them out in a field. Eager for the peanuts, the monkey stuck each hand into a jar, unaware that the necks would not allow his full hands to fit back through them. Had he dropped some of the peanuts from his hands, he would have been freed from the confines of the jar. But he wanted them so badly, he wouldn't release them. As a result, he was captured and sent away to live in a zoo. He wasn't willing to give up what was in his hands for what would have been better—his freedom.

We do this too. Our roles make us happy . . . in many ways they fulfill us and help us feel important. But they weren't meant to give us worth, and they create holes within us when we allow them to, whether or not they are taken away. In essence, we exchange our true value for one dressed up in a role. In order to keep our roles in their rightful place—loved, enjoyed, valued— we must never allow them to reign supreme in our hearts, convincing us that who we are is what we do.

My friend, anytime we give holes—in this case, being defined by our roles or identity—permission to rule in our hearts, we deny our place in God's story. This is hard for us to admit, because we have become comfortable operating with both our roles and our relationship to God. We typically evaluate the difference between the two only when we have been forced to do so, as was the case with my father and subsequently, with me. We may not have given outside sources approval to take things away from us, but we have the power to let the created purpose of our lives be the thing that we live, breathe, and exist for. We must understand that it is a most powerful and crucial choice, and we make it by acknowledging the limit to our roles and the limitless identity we have in Christ.

The choice to primarily identify ourselves with God

is the very thing that can make our soul well. I know this can seem like a complicated choice to make, because it causes us to dig deep and grapple with our desire to stay faithful to the roles we have been given. We feel that if we make something else more important, we devalue the other things we dearly love. In reality, though, when the thing that becomes more important is the thing that was intended to be just that—our primary, one-on-one relationship with God—our roles actually fall into balance. When He gave us our roles, He never intended that we confuse them for the people we are. He doesn't ask us not to love our roles; He just asks us not to let them take the place of Him.

I believe this is the reason, for example, Paul talks in 1 Corinthians 7 about the gift of being single. When other roles and relationships become primary, on the most basic level, they cause a distraction. Over time, they are often given priority. Eventually, they may even become first. This was not our created purpose. Romans 9:17 says, "I have appointed you for the very purpose of displaying my power in you and to spread my fame throughout the earth." But wrongly prioritizing our role can cause a breach between us and God—and nothing should be allowed to produce that. I'm convinced that in the moments we most want to hear from God, we have most forgotten to put Him first.

Holes in our roles are formed when we misunderstand our true identity, but they don't stop there—they
diminish the importance of our role as a child of God.
They can make us feel too important, causing an overblown sense of self. They can lead to deep insecurities
and feelings of inadequacy. I've seen a mom fall apart
over the fact that she did not make the cutest cookies in
her child's class for the annual Valentine party, and I've
seen a businessman define himself by his level of success,
both because of their dependence on their roles. I've seen
ministers plow aggressively forward to achieve attention
within their denominational circle, and I've watched
women dream of being the next big Bible study teacher,
just so they could rest in a role in which someone knew
their name. Our roles are beautiful. But they can't be our
link to life.

Getting Personal

You are probably wondering if in the story of my father
there is a part where he went to prison. The answer is:
both no and yes. I say no first, because in the primary
physical sense, he never had to go there. Though he was
charged and fined (large amounts of money) and put on
probation, by the grace of God he never had to spend
one day incarcerated. I am forever grateful, because the
life of those who are relegated to being locked behind

steel bars and the hell their family has to endure in their absence is formidable, and for a time this seemed a legitimate possibility for my father. But in another very real sense, he spent years locked in the prison of his heart. The shame and sorrow and difficulty he endured clouded his understanding of who he was in Christ, for a very long time. It is an understandable place to be, after the public loss of such a treasured role. And he was not the only one who felt it.

I, too, lost a role that night in 1994. I was the daughter of a pastor—a young adult woman who had never known anything but the role I had been born into. I loved the way my role felt. I cherished it. I didn't want it taken away, because it was all I knew. But it was not mine to choose to keep. Someone else made that choice for me, and I doubt they ever really knew what that decision meant to the others, like me, left in its wake. I didn't know either, for the longest time. It took me years to realize that despite the fact that I never had control over any of the decisions that changed my life through my dad's experience, I had all the power in my own life, through God's power within me, to choose for my soul to be well.

But before that, I would spend years wondering if people would ever love me for myself. It meant that I would search for my identity in other ways—many of them destructive, usually centering around relationships in which I felt I always had to prove my worth. The strong girl inside me suddenly became unsure, distant, and sad because I could no longer rest in my usual image of myself. Losing a position that had always been mine felt both cruel and confusing. Like my father, I struggled deep within for a time. In a very deep place, I recognized his pain.

Part of the spiritual recovery I mentioned in the previous chapter was my personal journey to understand who God wants me to be, outside of my roles. Looking back, I recognize it as one of the most important lessons of my life because it has allowed me to hold the things I love more loosely. Even now, I hesitate to assert that, because I know that I wear the flesh of all humans when it comes to people and things I love, and I fight the fear of losing them. But I also know that life is possible after roles are lost, and it can become even more beautiful. The level of the difficulty to live that statement relies heavily on the depth of how important those roles really are, some of which I do not fully understand. I know I cannot speak to the unspeakable: the loss of a role as parent or spouse. But having lived through my husband's extended job loss in recent years and my early experience with losing the most influential role of my young life, I can at least speak from an understanding for the road it takes to discover the truth about one's identity. At the end, it is a road of hope. I've traveled it, and I understand both its difficulty and its importance.

What about you? As you read this now, where are your roles positioned? What kind of power do they hold in your life? Do you love and appreciate them for the temporary roles that they are, or do they define your very identity? If they were to be taken without your permission, would you be left questioning your worth?

Holes in our roles are formed when we misunderstand our true identity, but they don't stop there—they diminish the importance of our role as a child of God.

I suspect that most of us live life never expecting our roles to be taken away. We are allowed to operate this way until something happens to change that status. It's a gamble most of us take, partly because we choose the simplicity of that thought over the more worrisome one (not in itself a bad strategy), but also because we are driven in our belief of the goodness of God to persuade Him to let us keep that which we have grown to love. But the reality of life is that though God is good—unequivocally, without pause or comma—life roles are not certain. We do not get to own what we get to enjoy, from the least of the important things, like money, to the most valued things, like family. God doesn't cruelly snatch those things away. But sometimes life does. In those moments, it becomes dire that we know who we are outside of them. Otherwise we struggle. Though our human condition will cause us to struggle anyway, the struggle becomes far greater when the core understanding of our identity in Christ is not firmly in place.

The holes of our identity can go very deep. They tap into the subterranean insecurities we have fostered inside for years—feelings that we are not good enough just by virtue of our created self. They make us spend too much time trying to figure out why. They make us try much too hard. They make us fall deeply in love with roles that should never become that important.

When It's Too Important

There are several stories I think of in Scripture where a role became too important. David's role as king became so important to him that he let it drive him to do things that were vile (see 2 Samuel 11). Once-fierce Samson became a lowly slave because he let his relationship with an evil woman cause him to compromise his created purpose (see Judges 16). Lot's wife's attachment to her beloved lifestyle made her desire it so much that she traded it for her very life (see Genesis 19). All of them

had free will and the same choices we have in life. Like
us, they could have chosen the thing that made their
soul well instead of things the holes of their identity
produced. But when roles become too important to us,
they cloud our judgment, cause us to compromise, and
even become our idol.

For men, one place this often shows up is in your job.
I've talked to many of my male friends and they attest
to this truth. Since at the Fall you were assigned to work
by the sweat of your brow, you assume that means that
work needs to define your worth. But God created your
work and your worth not to be mutually exclusive; you
can love and appreciate your work and work hard at
what you do, but at the end of the day, it cannot become
the only way you know how to define yourself.

There are plenty of working women who find identity in their work roles as well. But women hang on to
different roles much of the time. Women often gravitate
toward the nurturing wife and mother roles—even at
work—which makes sense, since we were born with
those instincts. Sometimes we, in a sense, fall in love
with other women in a way that becomes unhealthy—
a relationship of dependence in which we feel we need
others to complete us or validate our worth.

For both men and women, when a role changes
our path or replaces our relationship with Jesus in the

amount of time spent or efforts focused, it is a role that has become too important.

Moving toward Wholeness in Our Roles

I must admit, this book has made me look at a lot of things about myself, and sometimes they haven't been pretty. As I was preparing to write this chapter, I was forced to look at the holes in my own life in this area of roles and identity. I thought about the road of my recovery to understand that I was not a part of some created ministry package—some spiritual trophy to sit in a case and let people stare at its shiny exterior while its inner frame collected dust, even though for a time, its loss pained me. Some of my memories made me cringe (times I tried to fit in when I wanted to feel accepted), some of them made me cry (roles I made too important), but most of them made me feel grateful to be identified with Jesus in a relationship that could not be taken from me. I wonder if you feel this gratitude for His role in your life, or if you relate to my frailty of being so consumed with an earthly role that you have not been able to see that relationship as most important. Wherever you are, I hope you will remember His role in your life today, offering thanks for its constancy.

German Lutheran pastor, theologian, and martyr Dietrich Bonhoeffer once said, "If you board the wrong train, it is no use running along the corridor in the opposite direction."[4] This statement speaks such bold truth in relation to our roles and identity. If we've allowed our roles to become too important, we have boarded the wrong train. Everything else we attempt to do with a mistaken identity will be effort leading us down the wrong path; it won't fulfill the desires of our heart to be loved, accepted, and made well. The hinge moments may change our course. But our relationship with Jesus changes our life.

I know this: so many lost roles exist in the lives of the people who will read this book—so many beloved roles that matter to us so much. But though our roles may have produced holes within us, Jesus offers wholeness through it all. I envelop myself in that truth, as it is the thing that has fueled my hope for my lost roles to make me better. It is the truth that has driven the restorative portion of my dad's story as well, which I will share next. In one short moment in time, cowboy preacher Jim lost his church, his home, and his reputation. But he did not forever lose his soul. He did not lose his Jesus. Though his heart was once in prison, it was set free by the comfort that his relationship with God can never be taken from him. And it is the same for all of us. It is the thing that even our tsunami-on-crack moments cannot sweep away.

Questions to Consider

1. When have you experienced hinge moments of change with regard to a role, and how have those moments affected you?

2. Think of some of your most important roles in life. What would happen if one of them were stripped away without your permission?

CHAPTER 5

ROLES MADE WHOLE

This son of mine was dead and
is alive again; he was lost and is found.

LUKE 15:24, NIV

IN THE MUCK OF THE LOSS of my father's role as pastor, a couple of beautiful things emerged from all the ugly. One was about me. The other was about him. Both were about wholeness.

My beautiful-from-ugly experience, on a Wednesday morning not long after my father's resignation and subsequent day in court, was, in a word, surreal. There were many curious things about it, including why I had gone to chapel in the first place. The rebel in me kept me from many of those things that were expected but not required during my first year in seminary, chapel attendance among them. I loved the Lord, but I gave other things my time. But on this chapel day, with the experience of my father still so very raw, I was grieving many things. My instinct drew me to find comfort in the walls of a gathering of believers. After all, churches and chapels were places I knew so well, even if they now represented the place that had hurt me.

But in the glorious signature of God, His hand was silently at work when I couldn't see it. Stepping inside the theater-seated auditorium and finding my way to a seat beside several of my friends, I had no idea what would happen within the next forty-five minutes. The music started almost immediately, and I found myself questioning my choice to attend. I loved music, but today it just wasn't resonating with me. *Just brilliant, Lisa,* I thought. *You have way too much to do to be in here. Why today, of all days, did you decide to be a good girl and do what people want you to do?* I tried to remember the last time I had been there. I couldn't remember, not even one other time.

I looked two seats to my right, to a guy I had been out on a few dates with. I caught his eye and we smiled. A few more friends were scattered in front of me and behind. As the music came to a close, my mind fell in a methodical assembly line of what would come next: a welcome . . . a prayer . . . a grandiose introduction of our chapel speaker and his many accolades . . . and a forty-minute speech about how we could better serve God or something along those lines. I tried to be open to receiving something from this moment, yet the drill of spiritual programming and the pain of my recent experience kept threatening to shut tight the door to my heart. *This is just what church people do, Lisa. They tell you they care about you, then they throw you away. Why should you listen to them?* I sat still, reengaging in the moment just in time to hear the man on stage say things like: "Revered professor of something or other . . . been at the school for however many years . . . married with some-odd number of kids." By the time our speaker entered the stage, I had gone back to barely listening.

I'm guessing he was about ten to fifteen minutes into his message, based on the length of time it took me to draw my name in bubble letters on the paper in my lap and decorate each of their insides with varying crisscross, star, and swirly patterns. I finished my artwork and raised my face to try to listen. He was saying something about ministers and how easy it is to "forget our first love." I caught myself considering the truth of his statement; understanding how this could happen and had happened, even within my own spiritual experience. I had just decided to invest a bit more into listening when I heard him say these words to introduce the story he would use to illustrate his point: *"A well-known pastor in the Midwest . . ."*

My body completely froze, yet heat rose within. Immediately, the place above my upper lip began to sweat. I still do not understand and cannot explain why I so quickly and surely knew the story was mine, but I did, instantaneously, and all I could do was wait for him to tell it. I was embarrassed by the intimacy of its familiar details: *"The pastor of a large church lost it all . . . in a scandal over money . . . left his first love . . . hurt lots of people.*

I had heard many stories told in sermon illustrations in many sermons my father preached from many different pulpits. Now my life had become one. I wanted to stand up and scream, *"You don't know him. You don't know me. You don't know anything!"* But instead I sat, unable to move at all except for the blinking of my eyes as the tears fell into my lap.

I held my head steady and tried especially hard not to let my shoulders shake. In my periphery, I remember seeing my dating friend look over at me with a mix of puzzlement and curiosity on his face. He couldn't have known the story was mine—that the "well-known pastor in the Midwest" was the man I called Dad—though at the time I was sure he had to know. Even if he didn't, I was certain the people sitting behind me did, as they would have been able to see the large, imaginary sign on my back that said, *That guy he's talking about? Yeah, he's my father.* Embarrassment, shame, and anger all filled my heart over the story being told. I felt embarrassed that the story was attached to me. I felt shame that parts of it were true. I felt angry at the speaker for treating my family's story so callously. I couldn't believe I had put myself in a position that a man who knew nothing of my life could make me cry, all because I had willingly come to chapel to listen. Why, oh why had I decided to go on this day, of all days?

I didn't know the answers to anything. I just knew that every fiber of my being ached to make sense of the cruelty of the moment and the experience that had made me feel so vulnerable and exposed. My mind demanded to know why in the world God had been allowed to so coldheartedly forsake me when I needed Him most. My dad had lost his church. Both of us had lost our role. I didn't need any reminders of the experience that was now very deeply carved into my heart.

As I rushed out the doors before the last "amen," my instinct to receive comfort overwhelmed me. Where could I go to feel safe enough to watch my heart break? I found myself walking toward the office where I worked part-time as a proofreader for a silver-haired vice president named Dr. Jay. He had a commanding presence—fit, professional, and very tall—yet he felt grandfatherly to me, just as kind as he was put together. In the few months I had worked there, we had developed an easy, professional rapport. I knew Dr. Jay had been in chapel that day, because I had seen him sitting on the stage with the other vice presidents. I also knew that he was aware of the framework of my story. I felt safe, knowing he knew, though I did not know him well enough to know how he would receive me. Would he be busy, in an important meeting? Worse, would he be embarrassed that the young lady who worked for him in his office was marked by such a stain on the character of her family?

Those thoughts dissolved as I pushed open the heavy glass door to the reception area of his office. As I walked past my wooden desk on the right, I could see Dr. Jay through the open doors of his office a few feet away. He was standing there in his crisp business suit and tie with an expression of concern. Hearing me enter the reception area of his office, he lifted his face and his eyes met mine. I rushed into his open arms and fell to pieces.

I stood there sobbing into his blue pin-striped suit for at least a full minute. He did not speak. He did not move. He did not do anything but hold me. It was a catharsis I have rarely known in all of my life.

And then he simply said, "Lisa, I'm so very sorry."

I really didn't need for him to say anything else. What I needed he had already given me: comfort, love, compassion, understanding, acceptance, and the gift of his presence. I couldn't mistake the image he had made, arms extended from a long, lean frame: it was the perfect image of a cross. His arms represented the love I so desperately craved from my heavenly Father, letting me know I was still—always—His beloved child, no matter what other roles I filled or no longer filled.

My friend, that is the lesson of the lost role. That is the beauty in the journey of identity—that when roles no longer define us, because we lose them or put them in perspective, we find security in our sole identity with Jesus. We weren't created to attach to roles outside of God; we were created to enjoy them. The most amazing thing God ever does is allow us to be His child and love us just as much as He did the day He created us, even when we make other things in life more significant. In His goodness, He seeks to fill our empty space with a perfect love that brings completion to our soul. Losing our dependence on a role is the birth of true identity.

Until those other roles get out of our way, we cannot fully embrace our created role as God's child. We cannot know the depths of our purpose. We cannot feel the comfort of Him being enough. But with those other roles out of the way, we can discover those good things, which position us to live without fear.

Who we believe ourselves to be is so important. George Barna says in his book *Revolution*, "Your capacity to connect with God intimately and, therefore, to follow through on the challenges posed by the cause of Christ is inextricably bound to your self-image."[5] I could not agree more. It is not enough to identify ourselves with a group of believers, although certainly we are the created body of Christ, meant to live in fellowship with one another. But we must see our relationship with Him as primarily and intimately individual.

The truth is, the only hope we have of becoming anything at all in life is through the overcoming power of Jesus. Otherwise, we will chase things that won't matter in the end. We will feel abandoned and incomplete. We will cling to our roles and miss the purpose of life. Our souls will rot and wither in bitterness. On the other hand, wholeness gives us the capacity to value our roles in proper relation to who we really are in Jesus. That is where we will need to be when we find ourselves in our most vulnerable life-role moments.

Facedown

Often, before a breakthrough of wholeness, things look really bad. Such was the case for my father in the aftermath of his lost position. The first priority for Dad was to get his family away from the intensity of small-town scrutiny. With my older brother and me being grown adults and on our own, he had only to move my mother and young sister to a rental house in another state—a place at a drivable distance from him, so that on the weekends, Dad could be with his family. It was also a place where my family had both history and community, as it was in the town where my father had pastored another beloved congregation earlier on in his ministry. His other four days of the week would be spent living out on a piece of land he had hoped would one day be the site of a big, beautiful home for us, surrounded by plenty of the wildlife he had always loved. Having been forced financially to sell the family's current home in another part of town, his new home on the land had become a twenty-eight-foot camper. That's where he lived for a year, in a state of necessary, voluntary sabbatical for his soul.

I never really knew what kinds of things he talked to God about in that trailer or if he talked to Him at all. What I can tell you is that I spent many nights worried about the state in which he lived—spiritually, emotionally, and even physically. I didn't see him that often during that year—though we talked on the phone nearly every day. But while he was on sabbatical in a trailer out on a piece of land tucked back on a gravel country road in Missouri, I was in Texas at seminary, trying to recover from my own set of identity wounds.

I fiercely loved my father, though he had gravely disappointed me. But with parents like I had, it was not hard to extend grace, as it had always been modeled to me. As most children do, I spent some time personalizing his missteps, thinking of the ways I might have prevented him from walking into this land mine, though I never could come up with anything that would have made a difference. Mainly, I could not bear to see my father in such a desperate state, which is why I didn't visit him much. The one and only time I can remember going out to the land to see him, I felt physically ill. To see my once-charismatic father in a state of disarray and isolation was too painful—almost inconceivable. I didn't remember him this way, and I didn't want to. It troubled me too much.

The only thing I knew to do was to pray for him—consistently, earnestly, specifically. It is the burden I woke up with every morning and the responsibility that accompanied me to sleep. I prayed for him for months—long, tearful prayers in which I begged God to love him enough to help him have a breakthrough and see it. I wanted him to be whole, maybe even more than I wanted it for myself. I could not comprehend the thought of him going through his life not knowing how important he really was.

I clung to the thought that maybe, like Jacob, he was wrestling with God. It scared me more to think that he might choose to push Him aside forever and wind up in the same place that got him his *My Twisted Life* tattoo. I knew that if God could show him His law was covered with love, Dad could be convinced to come out of hiding. But I also knew that his critics were loud, especially the ones inside his head . . . and they could prevent that process from happening.

To this day, Dad has shared little of his time out on the land, and knowing him like I do, I assume that much of it is for my own emotional protection. But one thing I know is that the loss of his role hit him hard—harder than maybe any of us even expected. The lows were very low and there were few highs to balance them. Our family stayed together, though everything around us threatened to pull us apart. But we were driven to stand in the gap for a man who had so many times before taken care of us. God wouldn't throw him away, and neither would we.

My dad confided in me about one particularly poignant experience out on the land. The intimacy of it makes it a very difficult one to dredge up—even for me,

even now. Yet it is one he has graciously permitted me
to share.

It was a day at his lowest point, several months into
his sabbatical in the trailer. He had been isolated for
many days at this point, with just the weekend reprieves
to see my mother and sister. Few people in the town
reached out to him. It was as if he had literally fallen off
the face of the earth—an astounding contrast for a man
who had once been surrounded by gaggles of people
who loved him. He had begun to feel the effect of his
displacement and the rejection from his peers, many of
whom he had prayed with in hospital rooms, married
in beautiful candlelit weddings, or led to the Lord over
a coffee table—and all of whom he had fed the Word
through weekly preaching. Their silence in his greatest
moment of need was far too much.

Overwhelmed by the burden of this pain, my father
pushed open the trailer's coated metal door and walked
down its steep, narrow steps. As I write this, I can almost
feel movement of the trailer as the door slammed behind
him with the same intensity with which those manly
hands once gripped a pulpit. He walked out onto the
road that led to his portable home, looked out into what
had now become his life, knelt down, and did something
my mind will barely let me imagine. He pushed his
handsome face into the sharp, gritty covering of gravel,

and with swift back and forth movements he rubbed his flesh in its pieces. Cowboy preacher Jim had reached his lowest spot.

That day, I believe, the soul of a tarnished, broken man was purged out on a lonely strip of gravel, surrounded by silent trees. Maybe he cried out to God in that moment, or maybe he didn't. He never told me and I never asked. But what I am sure of is that seated in His royal place in heaven, Jesus saw it all, just as He had seen the day the man dressed in khaki sat at our kitchen table, the day my father resigned from his church, the day he held hands with my mother as they walked into court, and every other day that had come before. He was the same Jesus who had seen the young boy with toy guns in the living room, the teenager who found his way onto a Navy boat, and the young man who visited Pastor John in a brick Baptist church. He was the same Jesus who had seen the things that led up to this moment that were fair and just and those that weren't. And like many times before, His heart broke for His child who so desperately needed to know he would be okay without being anything but himself. He is the same Jesus whose heart breaks for each of us today.

I believe that in that moment when my father was facedown before God, a form of wellness began to grow. This wellness process—whereby he would be able to see himself in his true identity; feel unconditionally loved, accepted, and valued; and live without the limits of a role—is what I prayed he would experience then and it's what I pray for you to experience now. It is the process by which you choose the thing that makes your soul well, even if that thing is gritty and painful and extreme. It is an inner cleansing that happens when you let go of those definitions that have clouded your purpose and made you believe that in order to be okay, you must have them with you. It is the place the Prodigal had to go in order to recognize the richness that was already his.

The Road Back

I often think of the Prodigal Son—tired, messy, and feeling displaced. Luke 15 tells the beautiful story: A young man, driven by his impulses, longing to feel important, leaves his abundance behind and finds the world lacking. Eventually realizing his need to go back home, he is fearful of how he'll be received there. But his fears are unfounded. His father, driven by love, graciously opens wide his arms to receive him. It is the greatest image of unconditional acceptance I have ever envisioned.

Our road back to Jesus is no different. When we journey back to Him, He never turns us away—no matter the distance, no matter the span of time. Our journey back often involves a restoration of identity, as we tend to forget about our heritage when we are caught up in what we think we need to be. The fact that who we are is not what we do is something every one of us must understand and personalize to the depths of our soul. When we fully identify with God, we are able to appreciate the blessings of a Father to His child. The roles we enjoy are often such gifts, and God wants us to enjoy them, not idolize them. When we strike this balance, wholeness in our identity happens.

How do we achieve a balanced mind-set? On an individual basis and with a lot of earnest, faithful prayer. Often our desire for a quick fix leaves us wishing someone would write a formula to plug in for guaranteed change inside. Not only is that not entirely possible, but even if it were, it would also be detrimental to our soul. As we talked about in chapter 2, platitudes may sound good but they do not transform a heart. The truth is, if I could give you a formula, you might plug it in and never, ever change anything on the inside. Formulas don't take into account the unpredictability of life. They can't help you in those tsunami-on-crack moments when your roles—and all that goes with them—are stripped away.

What I can tell you is that when you're out of balance, getting facedown before God works. Facing hard truth works. Praying works. Reading the Word works. Choosing wholeness works. I know this because I have tried it both ways: practicing the formulas, never to have them change me; and doing the things that reconnected me with the heart of God, like searching for Him in quiet moments. The depth of a spiritual life is so simple that we mess up sometimes when we try to complicate it. Simply seek God. He will be found. ("If you search for him with all your heart and soul, you will find him," Deuteronomy 4:29.)

Falling down before God also helps in another respect: it keeps us from running away from the acknowledgment of our holes that brought us to the place where we most needed God. Many of us feel the nagging of these limiting places within and have tried patching efforts for years—busyness to deny the problem, formulas to follow spiritual rules, justification that we all live with limits—only to watch them fail. We become frustrated and feel let down when our roles don't reward our efforts by being enough. But laying them down before God is taking a step toward balance. It's movement toward great perspective and under-standing of meaning in life.

Our identifying moments change us because they help us realize that in Christ we are enough—without our roles, our dressings, our achievements. Though it took time, my father realized in many important ways that who he was—not a pastor or a father or a brother or a son or a neighbor or a deer-head broker, but a child of God—was enough. This man named Jim could exist outside of those roles, and he would need to. That would prove true many times after those roles were gone. It is what we all need proven true, and sometimes lost roles help make that happen.

Our completion is found in the arms of Jesus: we are enough because He is enough. But often, He does not *seem* enough for us because we don't give Him the time or space to be. We work Him in around all our other relationships and then we wonder why we can't feel His presence. We look for the quick fix that will satisfy our momentary urgings for relief or identity or acceptance—the praise of another or being the best at what we do. But change happens when we, the prodigal wanderers, leave those fleeting pleasures behind and come back home.

Maybe this is you and you are now traveling the road back . . . back to God and back to your core identity. If so, you are on the right path, as this path back will ultimately lead you forward. I don't suggest that you leave your roles. I just ask you to not let them define you. That is an important distinction, and it's one that can dramatically change your life.

Restoration

I wasn't the only one upset after that chapel service.
Despite my paranoia that everyone could identify me
as being connected with the chapel message, only less
than a handful of people actually knew the truth. But
at least one of those people called the professor's office
to let him know that not only was he speaking about
one of his own students, but that they weren't happy
about it. Much later that afternoon, I got a phone call
from a woman who identified herself as the assistant to
Professor Scott—the man who had spoken in chapel.
She asked if I would come in and meet with him at his
office the next morning.

I hesitated. Did I want to go meet with the man who
had rubbed salt in my open wound? Suddenly I felt like
I had some form of power, which felt good. I had been
powerless to stop the professor from telling my story, just
as I had been powerless to prevent it ever becoming a story
to tell. Now was my turn at control. I was tempted to
suggest that the woman tell Professor Scott "no" (and a few
other choice words) and hang up. But I agreed to go, with
an ulterior, fleshly motive. I would tell him that he hurt
me. I would make him feel ashamed. I would hear him say,
"I'm so very sorry," and it would make me feel better.

I walked into the professor's office the next morning

with great judgment, drawing conclusions about everything I could think of. *His chairs look stiff and cold and
hard. I bet he is a mean husband and doesn't make time for
his kids. He probably doesn't really love God.*

After a few attempts at basic conversation, Professor
Scott cleared his throat and leveled his gaze directly
into my eyes. I was surprised
at how awkward he now
seemed, away from the presence of the stage, though I
probably shouldn't have been.
I knew firsthand how people
who took stages were just
normal people, though they
carried the burden of living
up to a certain image. In

*Our identifying moments
change us because
they help us realize
that in Christ we are
enough—without our
roles, our dressings,
our achievements.*

many ways, it paralleled my own father's experience as a
pastor—ironically, the man Professor Scott had used to
make his sermon's point.

"I didn't know you were his daughter," he said.
"I would never have told that story if I knew you went to
school here. I want you to know that I've learned a great
lesson from this. I will never do this again, and I'm sorry."

I knew I needed to give a response, but I wasn't sure
what to say. I wanted to probe him about what part he
was most sorry for: that he had shared a painful page out

of my life while I sat right there in the audience, or that he had judged my father without really knowing him. In my pain I sought details, but the details ultimately wouldn't change anything anyway. It had felt good to hear him apologize, but not as much as I had thought it would.

"I accept your apology, Professor." My mouth said it, but my heart refused to relent just yet. I continued on with a question. "But may I ask where you got your information about my dad's story? Some of it wasn't completely true."

He paused, then answered, almost apologetically, "The newspaper."

I gulped hard, his words hitting a nerve. The media had been a great source of pain for our family during those difficult months. I was struck by how readily we can assume things based on someone else's words that might not necessarily be true.

"Well, sir," I said. "This may have just been a story to you, but this is my life. And your speaking about these things without understanding how it felt to really live them hurt me very deeply."

A few more words and moments later, the meeting was over. I walked out of his office and into the hot Texas sun thinking about the interaction that had just taken place. The professor had apologized, and I had

accepted. I had told him how I felt, and he had acknowledged it. There was really nothing more for either of
us to do than to move on from this difficult conversation, even though vindication was really what I craved.
But the kind of vindication I was chasing—one from
my inner grapplings with what was real and true about
ministry, love, and the sovereignty of God—was not
his responsibility to own. It was one I had to work out
privately with Jesus.

Restoration of identity is not a quick and easy one,
particularly when a role that has been dearly loved has
been taken away without our permission. This difficult
process is mandated to us by incredible circumstances
that disturb the parameters of our roles. Yet in some
ways, it is a better place to be than that of a person who
is still very ingrained in their role and sees no need to
change or become anything different. Comfort can be
a great deterrent; it has caused more than one person to
become limited. A man with a cancer diagnosis knows
he needs treatment. Though before he is fully aware
of the disease growing inside, he doesn't see a need for
medical intervention. Grasping the need to choose
wholeness in our roles, despite our present comfort,
takes knowing that the wellness of our life comes solely
from our relationship with Jesus.

If He can reach us while we are in our comfortable

state, He becomes our compass to guide us into remembrance of who we really are and what our lives are supposed to be about. I believe it is a place He tries to reach us first, as a desire to preserve one's child from pain is always the instinct of a loving parent. But the reality is that our flesh often prevents this process, requiring God to allow things to disrupt our life centered on our roles and let our circumstances prevent us from resting on anyone or anything but Him. He is the parent who loves His child enough to save us from ourselves.

Wholeness of identity is the most beautiful of all things that can happen within the heart of a believer. It restores simplicity to the Christian faith. It restores health to relationships and perspective to positions. It helps us hold more tightly to our intimacy with God and more loosely to everything else that might change. When we become desperate enough to desire no distance between ourselves and Jesus, we become motivated to give our roles a reprieve from the job of making us feel whole.

That will require getting facedown in front of Him and letting Him know that we are releasing our roles from their responsibility in our lives—not because it will affect them but because it will change us. It is as Abraham did with his beloved son, Isaac, in an unthinkable act of offering him as a physical sacrifice in Genesis 22—laying down something we love, even if in the end it is ours to keep. It is the choice to make Jesus most important.

And then, after the choice, the living comes in. Choosing what makes our soul well is not a one-time decision. In essence, it is the decision made every day of our lives, in one way or another. What does it look like to choose the identity, the role that makes our soul well? We define ourselves only by our relationship with Jesus. In marriage, we choose what will make our soul well when we love passionately but do not expect our spouse to provide our internal completion. At work, we choose what will make our soul well when we appreciate our position and give it our best effort but refuse to let it define our worth as a person. In our other relationships, including the great privilege of being a parent, we choose what will make our soul well when we value the gift of another in our lives and steward that position well but do not put the responsibility on it to hold us together.

I'd like to tell you that my dad didn't struggle after losing his role as pastor under a cumbersome cloud of suspicion, but he did. I'd like to tell you that for years—even after his original courtroom sentence—he didn't live with the stress of wondering if he would face a new charge and a possible term in prison, but I can't. I'd like to tell you that my mother, brother, sister, and

I all escaped this life event unscathed and with our faith in God and in the church unquestioned, but we didn't. I'd like to tell you that our roles weren't confusing and our hearts weren't broken, but I can't. All of that and much more happened. Choosing the thing that makes our soul well does not exempt us from the heartbreaks of life. But it does, in the end, change the course of what happens next.

The Real Story

There is a passage of Scripture I dearly love. It is taken from Joel 2, where Joel is prophesying to the people of Judah about the holes that had formed in their lives by their attachment to other things. At times it seems as if he is speaking out of both sides of his mouth as he talks of the judgment of God, then in almost the same breath, talks of His glorious intervention. But what that shows me is how fair God is, yet how deeply He desires to rescue, and how amazing it is that He can be both at the same time.

As Joel reminds Judah of who God is and what He has done, he uses beautiful word pictures to describe the power of His restorative hand. Some of the most powerful words come in verse 23 when he says, "For the rains he sends are an expression of his grace." I cannot help but think of the many rains that have come in the lives of those I love and how amazing it would be to have seen them as expressions of His grace as they poured down on them. Even now, I wish those rains away, forgetting that He often shows up most powerfully in them. The rains, even the most torrential, cleanse our hearts of the muck that makes us think we need something besides Him to complete us. Truly, it is an act of grace.

Often those rains bring believers into our lives at the time we most need to experience God. They come in and display aspects of His character—yes, including His great grace. As my father completed his time of sabbatical, there were people like that—those who were vitally important in the restoration of his identity with Jesus. A man at a church my father visited in those months and who knew his story shared with him this passage in Joel that now means so very much to me, telling Dad that he felt compelled to pray Joel 2:25 over his life, that God would "make up for the years of the locust" (*The Message*)—restore to Dad the years the destructive events had eaten away. How incredible is the thought that through a renewed intimacy with God, my father could get back the lost years of wandering around in a lost identity! How true it can become

Choosing the thing that makes our soul well does not exempt us from the heartbreaks of life.

for you, the sweetest days with Jesus being the ones yet to come.

Other people blew in with the rains in my father's life, people who believed in his worth and determined to model Jesus—men I will never forget for the wonderful way they represented my Savior. A young pastor named Wade, who drove hours to meet my father for lunch, not knowing that he

The rains, even the most torrential, cleanse our hearts.

would become a major catalyst for hope in his story. An old friend named Jay, who never stopped loving Dad and who might not have known how much one loyal friend mattered to a broken man. His big-grinned pastor friend, Harold, who gave Dad his pulpit one Sunday though he didn't have to, probably not knowing just how much his taking a chance on someone would mean to one who felt so undeserving.

In the coming years, Dad would go on to pastor a wonderful body of believers in a different state and eventually hold several other key positions within church leadership ministries. But his love for the great outdoors never lessened, nor did his desire to use the deer antlers he had managed to salvage from his collection for a ministry to men much like the cowboy Jim inside of him.

In what I can see in no other light but the divine,

this dream became a reality, and today his story involves reaching men with his newly expanded deer-head collection and a gospel presentation. From the fruit of this ministry he calls SOME—Sportsmen's Outreach Ministry Events—hundreds of men have been saved and changed who might otherwise not have come to Christ in a more traditional setting.[6] I cannot help but see the sweet paradox in his new ministry, as it loudly proclaims the goodness of God, His desire for ugliness to become radiant, and all things to come full circle in Him. Ironically, the very thing that once hurt my father the most—the combination of his two passions—was the very thing God used to help him heal.

It is the goodness of God to bring forth life from dead-ness . . . restoration from brokenness . . . growth from grace-filled rain. As Dad said one of the only times he has spoken publicly about his painful ordeal, "God was at the bottom, and He was waiting for me. He got me where I needed to be, at the point where He could break me and minister to me." It is true that at our lowest point, always . . . there is Jesus, waiting to remind us that life's richness is found in our community with Him.

In every story there are lessons. In your own life, you may be looking for yours. What was the purpose of a role you loved being taken away? Why did God create a yearning in you for a greater sense of identity? Maybe you even wonder, as I did for many years before my dad's church scandal occurred, whether in the sea of amazing stories you have heard other people tell, you have a story at all.

I assure you, my friend . . . you do. But it may not be what you think. It is not about your upbringing, your mistakes, or your successful climb to the top in your business, any more than my story is about what happened to my father that changed my role. Our stories are what has happened between Jesus and us which changed our lives.

The real story about roles—having them, loving them, losing them, missing them, wanting them, finding them—is the story of the person who finds their true identity in being a child of God. It is the story of the prodigal who walks the road back home. It is the story of the locusts and the grace-filled drops of rain. It is the story of the wholeness of Jesus, who makes all things, no matter what they are . . . well.

Questions to Consider

1. Has a hole in your life ever caused you to get facedown before Jesus? If not, what would it take

for you to get into that position, and how might that help you become whole within?

2. What would it mean for you to have your entire identity based on your relationship with Jesus? How could that become possible in your life?

CHAPTER 6

THE HOLE OF EXPERIENCES

Personally I am always ready to learn,
although I do not always like being taught.
WINSTON CHURCHILL

SOMETHING AMAZING HAPPENS when we begin to share about our life experiences: it creates a safe venue for other people to become brave. There may be no greater gift to give another than to admit that our journey has not been perfect, as the struggles of our life unite us far more than our successes ever will.

We each have a story. Our personal story can be a conduit for the message of Christ to flow from one life to another—the single greatest convincer to the world that Jesus is real. But the biggest snag that message can hit is when we make our experiences (both good and bad) our story. We have to understand: our story is what happens between Jesus and us in the pages of our earthly journey. Our experiences are the circumstances in our life that shape us along the way. Holes are created when we allow those experiences to become our story. Understanding those three elements of our life—*our story, our experiences, and our holes from those experiences*—will allow us to see our experiences for what they are instead of allowing them ownership in our lives. It will also help position us to thrive with Jesus and live out our life purpose. Without this understanding, our story is relegated to the facts of our life. And those hold only the power we give them.

Story versus Experiences

For the believer, our complete story—*what happens between Jesus and us in the pages of our earthly journey*—is our greatest vehicle for showing people the God of transformation. This is what the prophet Samuel spoke about to Saul when anointing him as king in 1 Samuel 10:6: "The Spirit of the LORD will come powerfully upon you . . . you will be changed into a different person." When we encounter Jesus and He changes our life, our story holds transformative power that goes way beyond our own ability to change.

The ironic thing is that many of us do not really

know what our story is, so we either share nothing at all or we pick the experience that had the most impact and slap a "my story" label on it. We may feel discouraged when we hear the amazing experiences of another—one where they overcame great odds or survived beyond expectation—and we think to ourselves, as I thought for much of my life, *I don't have a story.* The problem with seeing our story as the horribly painful moment that most impacted us, or even as the best, happiest, or most successful moment of our life, is that often, we become defined by it. But the amazing effect of seeing our story as what happens between Jesus and us on our earthly journey is the opening up of equal opportunity for every believer to share, and share powerfully.

Scripture underscores this truth in the opening verses of Acts 4, where we find Peter and John preaching to the people on a bit of a controversial subject: the resurrection of the dead. A Jewish sect called the Sadducees didn't like what they were hearing, particularly because it directly refuted their belief that such a thing did not exist. Because of their position they were allowed to arrest the men and throw them in jail. They then questioned Peter and John about their bold teachings and were met with an equal amount of boldness from the disciples as they answered, compellingly, about Jesus.

Perhaps the greatest impact Peter and John had that

day was on the Sadducees themselves, though that group would have been among the last to admit it. They knew that the two men were unschooled and recognized them as being empowered by Jesus, as "they could see that they were ordinary men who had had no special training" (Acts 4:13). I imagine they were a bit freaked out and a little more than worried

Our story is our greatest vehicle for showing people the God of transformation.

by this finding. Even they knew that going up against such spiritual power—the supernatural power of God that spoke the world into existence, calmed seas, defied death, and changed lives through His simple touch—could prove difficult.

What affects me most about this passage is the evergreen reminder that ordinary people can be empowered to do extraordinary things. This is important to remember as it relates to our story: when we are limited by the holes our experiences produce, we stifle this ability, which is what often leads to discouragement. Peter and John were great guys and had been disciples of Jesus, but in order to do something so courageously insane as to sit in a jail cell and challenge the people who put them there, they would have to have more than mere guts. In fact, in their story you can see the theme that runs in the lives of all people we see doing remarkable things for God: the ability to carry off what is not otherwise possible because of a supernatural empowerer.

The potential to have that kind of limitless, thriving service for God—one in which we represent the power He has to use any of us in a supernatural way—lies within all of us as believers. One person's story will look different from everyone else's, because we are all individually created. The sharing of our story does not require Bible college training, conference attendance, or weekly classes at church. It is not for someone else to determine for us, and it does not require that we have a massive audience or platform. It simply requires the remembrance of what has happened between Jesus and us on our earthly journey and the willingness to share that experience with someone else.

Our gifts allow us unique ways to share the story. Our passion for what that story means to us is what will influence the world to want to know our Lord. The only thing that will stand in the way is how much power we allow our experiences to hold over us. Peter and John could have confused their experiences (being thrown in prison while doing ministry) with their story. Had they done this, they would have either taken it as a sign that they should quit the ministry or overblown their importance in the bigger-picture story of Jesus. But they knew innately that their story was all about Him, and it fueled them.

Experiences are different. They are not our story but rather the circumstances that shape us along our journey. In saying this, I want you to know that I am not in any way diminishing the magnitude of your experiences by using the word *circumstances*. Circumstances can be massive. They can be life-altering. Even the accumulations of our smaller circumstances have the ability to shape us in many ways. But in the scheme of our story, they are simply support characters.

Both positive and negative experiences can bend us out of shape when we allow them to become too important. On the positive side, we desire the successful experiences of life—and this in itself is not a bad or misguided desire. A businessman who determines to succeed may well be operating under the "do all to the glory of God" model and therefore his best pleases Him and does give Him glory. But of course the same businessman's success—positive experiences—might be bringing glory only to himself. If this happens, it can lead to a hole of pride or self-sufficiency, whereby Jesus is excluded from his story. Both things are true: we are created to do great things, but we cannot do great things of lasting importance without God.

Negative experiences and how they shape us are

much more easily accessed in our mind, though often we spend some portion of our life actively attempting to block them out. But when negative things happen to us, they leave an imprint on our psyche. I've heard this described before as sustaining a burn on the skin, which causes us to walk around in a constantly raw state. It's the reason certain people rub against us like sandpaper, triggering things in us that we don't quite understand, or why we sometimes react more strongly than a circumstance really warrants: we are highly sensitive to our negative experiences and they color our responses.

The truth is that most life experiences are entwined with elements of both the positive and negative. A lot of us can look back on our experiences and see how they changed us, both in ways we didn't want them to and in ways that made us stronger. It is how I would characterize the experience my husband and I had in planting—and closing—a church, all within a period of about thirteen months.

One Shaping Experience

First, I must tell you that this was not something either one of us ever thought we would do. We never saw ourselves in the role of lead pastor and his wife, and to be honest, after what I had already experienced with my parents in their church ministry, everything within me resisted the idea. In my mind, I didn't need the church to give me another reason to go to therapy.

But even though I had married a man who was straight from the halls of seminary, I rested in the fact that my husband was an outside-the-box thinker and was not compelled by the belief that the only true "ministry" is that done behind the podium of a church. We started our marriage in nonprofit ministry by launching a local chapter of a national public school campus strategy meant to empower students to reach others for Christ on their campus—so leading a church did not seem very likely, much less starting one.

But that's exactly what we found ourselves doing fourteen years later. In all that time—and for many years prior to that, on our own—we had worked in the church as laypeople. Except for a few intern or contract positions sprinkled in, this defined our service to the church. I did women's ministry and he helped with the students and eventually taught a large Sunday school class. We both worked in the children's area, and my husband coached kids' sports and went as a counselor to student camp. Our love for the church showed in the way we served it—not always perfect, but always driven with a passion to serve Jesus well.

In the course of two years, as we watched God exceed our expectations in the explosive growth of our small group Sunday school class, our passion grew to attempt something even bigger for Him, though we weren't sure exactly what. People had talked to us for many months about the idea of starting a church, and though we appreciated their passion, we were at first adamantly closed to the idea. We felt the task too big for our abilities, particularly because of our already incredibly busy and stretched life. With my writing and speaking schedule, our growing children, and my husband's very demanding job as the Vice President of Operations of our family business, our life was already full to the brim and on some days, spilling over. We knew that starting a church is not something one simply squeezes in.

But as the months went by and the urgings continued, we gave the idea of starting a church careful consideration and prayer. The large church we were a part of knew of our passion for helping the Kingdom thrive and the leadership prayed with us for God's way to become known. We did not want to miss God, and we felt He might be using the voices of others to prompt us to do a wider-scale Kingdom work. What we knew was that we (especially my supersocial husband) loved people and that we wanted to be open to serving God in whatever way He wanted. All the signs were adding up for us to branch out and start a church: we were praying; we were seeking the counsel of others; we had a strong scriptural grounding of what the church should be; my husband was a strong, effective communicator; we were a united team; and we were successful in our current efforts and in building a great support structure around us.

So with a lump in our throats and a passion in our hearts, in April of 2009 we launched Thrive Church. We spent weeks leading up to it gathering our support team. We earmarked Acts 2 in our Bibles and referred back to it often, solidifying our core beliefs on what church should look like based on that, in addition to our ministry training and lay experience. We even spent time thinking about what it would look like in the aesthetic sense, too, poring over logo design and picking out our signature "Thrive green" color. We had such a strong belief that God could do something amongst us that was organic and natural, building the church and reaching our city.

It was both beautiful and difficult from the very start—with both positive and negative experiences interlaced. We had a wide range of responses to our decision, ranging from great opposition to great support, but none of it defined us. After many earnest prayers, we had done what we felt was right and good and would make a difference, and it is what drove us.

The beautiful part of the experience was the people.

The support of the community of people who loved and believed in Thrive Church as a movement of God blessed us and fueled our passion for greatest-commandment living: to love God and love others. They labored right alongside us, doing things none of us had ever done before. We stayed up late, set up chairs, hauled sound equipment, prayed, laughed, and cried together. We read the Word, shared meals, and talked about doing more for God—all aspects of the amazing early church movement in Acts. We were blessed by seeing how, even down to its final days, the experience stretched all of us and yet pulled us all together.

The difficult part was everything else. With our already-busy schedules, the time we hoped to have to pour into this new work of God did not exist. The little time we did have we hoped would eventually develop into much more, as our desire was always to commit to the work full-time as it grew. We launched with nearly one hundred people, so with that core group being quite large, the needs were great from the very beginning. We cared deeply for the needs of the people, but our lack of time prohibited us from being present in the way we wanted or they needed us to be.

From the start, we were incredibly bogged down with details. Whereas we launched the church with the desire to minister to the people in a deeper way,

we found ourselves spending time and energy dealing
with the details of venue, schedule, sound and lighting,
and all the other usual logistical aspects of early church
works. This ate away at the time we had to dedicate to
the people and the areas of the church we wanted to see
live up to its name. All of this led to frustration, both
on our part and on the part of the people who believed
in us and the work of Thrive Church. We worked
through months of borrowed time, sleepless nights,
venue changes, sermon series, late-night meetings, and
seeing people we loved come and go before my husband
and I had the tearful conversation one night that led to
the close of our beloved endeavor. The end of Thrive
Church came almost exactly thirteen months after the
day it started. The decision to end it was excruciating
in nearly every way.

The relevance of this life experience is not in
considering why we decided to open a church that we
then, only months later, closed . . . though certainly
there were many lessons learned along the way.

In the end, it came down to doing what was best for
everyone involved with Thrive Church, including our
family. We knew that our service to God wouldn't end
with this work, but our effectiveness there couldn't exist
without a full-time effort—one which we had prayed
to see happen for over a year but never did. We stopped

Thrive as we had started it: with consideration, seeking counsel, and getting on our faces before God. And even though starting a church is a major undertaking, what this experience has in common with all other life experiences is that it shaped us in both positive and (for a time) negative ways.

Despite the fact that the church was short-lived, there had been many positive experiences. For one, the partnership between my husband and me and our desire to do ministry together and in creative ways was strengthened. Our marriage was strengthened beyond anything we could have ever imagined, and so was our faith. We had seen people get saved and had experienced the privilege of pouring ourselves into lives and watching them change through the power of God. And we had come to a better understanding of what the church is supposed to be and what it is not. Our eyes were opened to the great ministry that happens in many different places, with many different people, in pockets all across the world, many of them going beyond the walls of the church. It was painful to close the door on that intense period of awareness and growth.

On the negative side, we had disappointed a lot of people. In the course of doing a new work together, some important friendships were strained and some even severed. We had faced judgments that hurt us. Some people lost confidence in our ability, both to hear from God and to lead His people with true vision. We began to question those abilities as well. And we struggled with the decision to quit something we had started or fail at something we had attempted.

We made a leadership decision that was hard, like many leadership decisions we had to make in the thirteen months before, though none had been quite so piercing. We were hyperaware that either decision we made held its own set of consequences: either we could continue doing something we were trying to do on borrowed time and risk jading our beloved people about how effective ministry is done, or we could shut down the church, help them feel released to go to another work to be better led and nurtured, and risk facing their opinion and judgment. Neither option felt particularly good though I had seen firsthand with my father's experience what might happen if we continued to do too many things—even good things—at once.

Within the difficulty, there was an undeniable measure of peace. That is how we knew our decision to end this experience—no matter how much we loved it— was right. It was the decision we knew would ultimately make our souls well, and those of our congregation— and that's the bottom line. Regardless of the different details of your shaping experiences and mine, it's how we choose to let them affect us that really matters in the midst of our experiences.

When we allow the emotions stemming from our experiences to rule over us, defining our journey, our souls suffer and we cannot enjoy the precious gift of His peace.

Holes from Our Experiences

What I'm about to say may surprise you, but it may also give you hope: your painful experiences may be no more detrimental to a thriving life than your joyful ones. It's not difficult to believe that our difficult experiences can keep us from living our purpose and thriving at it. But the truth is, all experiences—positive and negative— have the potential to create holes within us. What I'm referring to is the delicate life balance between under- standing, appreciation, and ownership.

We can understand and appreciate our experiences for what they are, but once we allow them to own us, they limit us. Some of you know about this firsthand, as you have lived a portion of your life with your experi- ences owning you. I can relate to this. In the experiences with my religion leading up to my spiritual recovery, the circumstances with my father's role and my own, and then this experience with Thrive Church, all of them once threatened to own me.

Here's the thing about ownership: when you own something, you decide what to do with it. I will never forget the house where I used to live in a town in Texas when I was in seminary. It was the ugliest shade of pink I had ever seen. People used to visit the street it sat on just to gawk at its ugliness and talk about how crazy the owner must be to have painted his house that particular shade of Pepto-Bismol pink. But it was *his* house. He owned it. So he could do whatever he wanted with it, including painting it the color he liked that everyone else hated.

Ownership brings the kind of power that, under its authority, can paint houses ugly shades of pink and cause people to live their lives limited by their experiences. When we allow our experiences to own us, they limit us and make us feel powerless to their control. When our experiences have power, they are allowed to become our story, which produces holes. But we own our experiences; they do not own us. This understanding puts the power back in our hands

It was the decision we knew would ultimately make our souls well, and those of our congregation—and that's the bottom line.

to choose how much they will influence our life. It's a beautiful thing to know and one that will result in great and lasting freedom.

In a very real way, our experiences can become things of idolatry. They can consume great masses of our time. We can put too much energy into them. We can depend on them instead of God. And when that happens, they can become debilitating—or cause us pride. They can become idols. At times, our experiences with Thrive Church threatened to give it that kind of idolatrous power over me.

Many stories in the Old Testament illustrate the great harm in idol making. In particular, I think of the story in Exodus 32. In the absence of their fearless leader, Moses, the fearful Israelites beg Moses' brother and assistant, Aaron, to give them something else to follow, and he obliges. After melting down their gold offerings, he molds an image into that of a calf and they promptly begin to worship it. The Lord is angered by their idolatry—in the worship of something other than Himself—and only holds back the unleashing of His anger because Moses asks Him to. How much like the Israelites we often are, making things more important than God. Even our very own experiences.

Moving toward Whole in Our Experiences

As we come to the close of this chapter, I have a pair of questions I'd like you to really consider. Was there a moment that your life took a turn? If so, what was it?

I want you to spend some time on this, because identifying these moments can lead to a great understanding of the experiences that may have limited you. The reality is that we are less likely to repeat patterns that led us to holes if we identify where those holes first came from. I would love nothing more than for you to start identifying these things for yourself, even today.

Some things to keep in mind: It may be multiple things that have altered your course or impacted your life. It may be something hugely positive that you welcomed or something harshly negative that you wished to reject. As with our experience with Thrive Church, it could be a combination of the two. Maybe it brought you turmoil, or maybe it brought you joy. Consider the question with regard to God, your other relationships, living out your life purpose. Did it make you feel most important, or cause you to experience lingering negative feelings, or marginalize your relationship with God? If it did, my friend, it has become a hole.

The good news is that even if it has, this is not the end of the story. It may well be, in many ways, just the beginning. Thrive Church was certainly a shaping experience, in nearly every area of our life. Closing it was excruciatingly difficult, even though we had peace and experienced a level of relief from the weight of its responsibility. I felt guilt, shame, and regret—all those same things I felt during my early years with the church and in moments like the one with my camp speech, when I felt like a fake and phony but wished to be spiritually real. In circumstances like these, it required some drilling down and getting honest—laying it all out before God and asking Him to make sense of the aftermath of my stormy experiences. My experiences will forever stay in my heart's memory, but they aren't allowed more value than the bigger story I have with Jesus. They are simply a chapter in my earthly journey book.

In the same way, your shaping experiences, no matter how significant they may be, do not define you. They can't be allowed to hold so much power that they hold you back from your created purpose. They are a sentence, a paragraph, a page . . . maybe even a chapter in the story of your life. The bigger story you have is with Jesus. He is waiting for you to let that story become most important. It is the time He will meet you to fill up those empty, limiting holes in a way that only He can.

I love His promise of this in Psalm 126:5, that "those who plant in tears will harvest with shouts of joy." Shouts of joy from tears that are deeply rooted in our hearts can only be possible through the healing of Jesus: the God who makes all things well. It is with that truth in mind that I am able to believe that any and every circumstance in our life can become a great place of wholeness where great joy and peace are found. *Any. Every. All.* Even those most dire or difficult.

There are so many amazing people who have far more monumental life-shaping experiences than I do, many of which I have had the privilege to hear as I've been in this capacity of ministry. People have shared some incredible ones with me: stories of lives that had been wrecked but that Jesus salvaged, as well as those whose experiences led them to become prideful and destructive. I know you have such stories of your own, or of those who are close to you, that you could add in—so many experiences of so many incredible things are represented in the lives of believers sharing space on earth. But it all comes back to the bigger picture, of which these circumstances are only a small part: His desire for us to experience His way of wholeness in the story of our life.

Questions to Consider

1. Do you see the importance of making a distinction between your story and your experiences? Have you been making your experiences your story? How might doing so facilitate a hole?

2. In what way(s) can a positive experience still create a hole? Can you recall a time in your life when that has happened and how it limited you?

CHAPTER 7

EXPERIENCES MADE WHOLE

The world breaks everyone,
and afterward, some are strong at the broken places.

ERNEST HEMINGWAY

PEOPLE FASCINATE ME—their courage, their difficulty, their giftedness, and their perspectives. How vast all of it is, with so many of us occupying earthly space. I'm especially moved by people who are able to dig into the dirt of their humanity and look squarely at the ugliness beneath what appears beautiful. The truth is, sometimes the most powerful thing we can do is to accept something when we wish it had been something different. To me, this is real life: accepting our struggles while operating with hope, achieving without losing our souls. This kind of living demonstrates the kind of life offered by

Jesus, who dazzles us even in our most difficult moments and makes all our earthly successes pale in His greatness.

As I wrote this book, I thought about you. I tried to picture your circumstances, what's written on the pages of your life. I realize I can't know your journey so far, but I try anyway. Maybe it's what I have been through in my own life that lets me know that no matter how different our circumstances may be, we each live and lose and love and cry and work and let go and endure and break down and get back up. It is the universal tie that binds all of us together, and it matters deeply. I know that the fullness of how we love each other as human beings is in our understanding of how similar we really are, and how much we need each other to care. We truly were not meant to take this journey alone. God knew that we would often need the physical presence of another to buoy us up, and for that I am grateful. In my own life, it has often been the comfort of another that has been the greatest earthly picture of the kindness of God.

What I most want you to know is that it is possible to have wholeness despite your experiences—in fact, right within them—no matter how significant they are to your heart. Where this is not possible in the flesh, in our own strength, it is ever possible in the Spirit. We are futile in our efforts to be well without Him, as it says in Psalm 127:1: "Unless the LORD builds a house, the work

of the builders is wasted." God's design has always been
that we would need Him to do that which we cannot.

Perhaps some of our past difficulty in becoming
whole in the midst of our experiences is due to our
efforts to try to do so by strong will or determination.
We do need those aspects of inner grit. It has been
famously said that life is 10 percent what happens to us
and 90 percent what we make of it, which gives the nod
to our capacity to emotionally conquer the experiences
of our life by our reaction to them. I believe that is true.
I also believe we often need the perspective and wisdom
of another in this process and can greatly benefit from
counselors, mentors, pastors, even trusted friends who
listen well. But I believe it takes Jesus to truly make that
possible in a lasting, completed way.

When His power within us, as opposed to our own,
is at work, we gather insight from our experiences,
strength and courage, a new level of understanding, a
new transference of grace, and the discipline required
to become more than what has happened in our
lives—good and bad. As Jesus said, "In all these things
we are more than conquerors through him who loved
us" (Romans 8:37, NIV). All these things: the good
things, the bad things . . . the things we didn't ask for
and never wanted, the things we wanted but never
got . . . the things that left us with gaping holes, that

we thought we couldn't get past. All these things are possible to be conquered. They only require Jesus. The most brilliant part of that is, He is always available.

Waking Up

There's something that happens to you when you wake up from a difficult experience and realize you are still breathing. Just as a colorful bud on a flower defies the weight of the heavy mound of snow it's buried under to show signs of spring, so does the breakthrough of a new day prove its viability despite life's deep complications. The decision, then, is whether or not to welcome it, and I've found it often depends on the depth of the pain and the length of time we have allowed it to reign in our lives. But as Helen Keller once said: "Although the world is full of suffering, it is also full of overcoming it."

I woke up one morning after the shutdown of our church to the sound of my own labored breathing. I still remember the feeling. *I can't believe I survived this*, I thought, hardly able to process what had happened over the preceding thirteen months. It was not unlike the way I felt the morning after I realized my father was not going to prison over his financial discrepancies with the IRS.

As I lay in bed thinking back on many things, I welcomed the sight of my hands resting lazily on the covers that were pulled up to my neck. It was a sign that shutting down the church, though excruciating, had not succeeded in completely taking me down as I had feared it would. One of the great ironies of life is that in the midst of pain over what once was and now isn't, there can be joy in the gift of finality—even when it is something we really wanted to hold on to. Finality can mean the end of some of our worst nightmares. The unshackling of the prison of our definitions

God's design has always been that we would need Him to do that which we cannot.

and the scourge of our internal critics. The release from pain—years of it; weeks of it; days, hours, or seconds of it—however long it's gone on, that is a moment too long. Shutting the door to the stigma of our past experiences is opening the door to the limitlessness of our future possibilities. In that way, finality can be welcome, because it symbolizes a new day of wholeness. This is truly a thing of joy.

Yet I know that there are people who wake up from experiences to realize they are still breathing, and they aren't sure they want to be. This is a place of darkness I do not know personally, although I believe it is a real place and one where any one of us might find ourselves someday. But without our consent, most of our experiences do not take the breath within our body. Instead, they leave us breathing, passing to us the baton of decision. No matter the depth of pain or the difficulty of circumstance, no matter how much choice we have over what is happening to us, it is within our power to choose how to face what comes next: our future. One of the gravest mistakes we believers can make is when we forget that our circumstances limit us only if we allow them to.

My prayer today is that you are waking up from the experiences in your life, craving that new day and having a hopeful new perspective on your future. Your life can be better—better than what already seems amazing and rich and full . . . better than what is painful. We all have the opportunity to thrive, which is the promise of Jesus. Despite what some worldly scholars may say, we are not able to accomplish this through human efforts of self-actualization: "Not that we are sufficient in ourselves to claim anything as coming from us, but our sufficiency is from God" (2 Corinthians 3:5, ESV).

You and I were meant to need God desperately, so we do. We can't manage ourselves well enough to have right perspective on our experiences, so we must have His. The great incongruity of the Christian faith is our ability to live in the sludge of the world while focusing on the brilliance of what comes after. The Jesus who makes all things well—and only He—makes this possible.

Moving Past

God is bigger than all our man-made messes. I cannot tell you how thankful my belief in that statement makes me. When you screw up as often as I do, you're that much more thankful for an all-access God who has no ability to make mistakes and yet infinite capacity to handle ours. I am convinced that a layer of our spiritual facade is peeled off when we appreciate the difference between our personal weakness and the steady strength of Jesus Christ. Time and again I have listened to people talk about the things and people that have hurt them and how but for the presence of God in their life, they might otherwise have ended up in a ditch. Their testimonies remind me that the only way to survive the brutal outcome of living in a fallen world is to focus intently on a relationship with the one trustworthy God.

My friend Angie can attest to this, and unfortunately her story is all too familiar. When her father left her, she felt utterly and devastatingly abandoned. She waited by the phone and sat at her living room window daily, wishing her daddy would make his way back home. She lived with this wish for years until she finally gave it up. It took mounds of time for her to even begin to process this loss, and to this day she does not fully trust men. Her experience has taken its toll on every other male relationship of hers, and as a result, Angie's trust in a heavenly Father has not come easily either.

But over time, Angie's belief in God has strengthened. Every time He did not walk away when she shared her deepest feelings, she gave Him more access to her heart. Every moment He did not give someone else priority over her and cause her to feel less preferred, she gave Him more time. She had gone to places dark and lonely, and He alone went there with her. Angie's attachment to the Savior she had already professed increased with every earthly letdown she experienced, including ones from her very own religion. And in the end, she was left with a deeper, more abiding and intimate relationship with God. Wholeness rises from the ashes of our experiences when we cling to the God who makes it possible.

This type of depth is similar to what can happen in a marriage relationship over time. I've watched my own parents' love for each other grow deeper and fuller with every year they have journeyed together: forty-six years and counting. Marriages do not always turn out this way, and if a union does make it that long, you know it was not without its moments of struggle between two imperfect humans trying to coexist in daily living. But as much as marriage may be the context for disappointment, it cannot be denied that God crafted the perfect prescription for love, faithfulness, companionship, and even accountability in this idea of marriage. It's not that the concept doesn't work. It's that we are lacking in the execution of it.

Even in my own fifteen-year marriage (that has, itself, been full of great ups and downs), I recognize the parallels. At home not long ago my husband stopped in front of a set of eight-by-ten pictures of us on our wall—one of us at our wedding and one of us taken almost fifteen years later. He paused for a minute; then, with his back to me, pointed to the picture of us now and said, "I like us better here." I smiled, catching what he meant, but I couldn't help think about why, in many ways, things had been better then. Certainly, in our young, blissful state they were much easier. So what was the improvement?

It isn't that we look any better now or that our bodies are in the same shape. It's that while the picture from our wedding represents two young, vibrant twentysomething people with big dreams, the picture of us now represents two people who have come to better understand what a true partnership is all about. The young couple in the wedding picture didn't have a clue how to put the other first. They didn't know how to love someone through a difficult moment because they had never before weathered any as a couple. But the couple we are now has seen some heart-wrenching days. We are familiar with what happens when one or both of us decide to be selfish. We know what it is like to want to run away from a problem, yet be drawn back to sift through honest feelings of our unmet expectations. Those are the kinds of things that create the depth that people like my parents continue to experience, some silver hair, capped teeth, bad knees, and forty-five years later.

That is the kind of depth we can have in our relationship with God. He has seen us in our most downright ugly, selfish, and hard-to-deal-with states, and He still offers us His great love. When we realize this, especially during difficult life experiences, our desire for a deeper relationship with the One who knows our hearts naturally grows.

Depth that comes from wholeness from our experiences manifests itself in ways other than relationship as well. It is depth of understanding that we call wisdom—spiritual insight—as well as a realignment of our perspective. Jesus extends this depth within the offer of His wholeness. It is a by-product of having Him fill our holes to make us well within.

Seeing Things Clearly

One of the hardest things to do with our experiences is to allow them to live between the guardrails of perspective. So often, they threaten to break out of the safety and stability of protection to the open shoulder of the road of life, where emotions are allowed to run free. This was what happened to me, for a time, during our experience with Thrive Church, in the weeks before we finally decided to close it.

The church had been in existence for about nine months when we found ourselves at the breaking point. My husband and I were barely hanging on, in nearly every sense. Though we still had a core of people gathering with us, many of *them* seemed to be barely hanging on, too, frustrated by our dwindling accessibility. The church didn't have the funds to sustain us full-time, and the family business Scotty was running wasn't sustaining us either. His construction business had taken a hard hit with the crash of the housing market, so the position we had been in when we started the church was not where we were now. Most months we got paid nothing from either venture. But beyond that, because Scotty had to reengage in the business in ways he had not anticipated just to keep things afloat, we became so distracted by the suddenly overwhelming needs of our personal life that we were no longer as available or even as inspired, and we weren't thriving in our own lives because we had taken on way too much.

One particular day I was feeling very low. The weight

of all of my many responsibilities, all the people I was sure we were letting down—including our friends, each other, our kids, and most of all, God—rested squarely in the middle of my chest, stifling my breathing. The burden of all the things I wasn't doing well and all the things I felt I couldn't control overwhelmed me. Entombed by my own self-judgment, I wept.

I took my weeping into the after-school car line, as I was on taxi-mom duty that particular day and had to pick up a load of schoolkids, including my own. On the way out the door, I absentmindedly picked up a pile of mail that had been sitting on the counter from my mailbox run earlier that day, not noticing anything in particular. I set it down on the seat next to me and cried myself all the way to my children's school.

Within minutes I arrived at the school and found my place in the long line of other taxi-mom and -dad cars, waiting my turn. I was grateful for the silence of the car but overly conscious of the people who might see me wiping my eyes and wonder what horrible tragedy had happened to Lisa Whittle that had made such a strong woman cry. Then paranoia overtook me, as I automatically felt misunderstood by their judgments—the perceived judgments of people who might not have even seen me yet. My ugly flesh was making me a mess.

These were tears of sadness, but also of anger. I was

angry at the unforeseen circumstances that came along and prevented us from leading the church well. I was angry at the people who had asked us to start the church, then left us within months, and at those who hadn't chosen to support us in the first place. I was angry that we couldn't do it right and that it made me feel incompetent. I was angry that phrases like *not enough*, *need more*, *can't do*, and *overworked and exhausted* even existed and, worse, applied to us.

Most of all, I was angry with God. I was angry that He hadn't helped us do this thing well when I knew He could blink and it could be successful. I was angry that He had allowed us to do something that I told Him I never wanted to do in the first place. I was angry that He apparently loved other church planters more than us because they had flourished and we hadn't. I was angry that there was obviously a lesson He wanted us to learn and that in the process, He had chosen not to bless our work. It was clear. Barring a miracle, we were going to fail. Short of God's intervention, we were going to have to shut down this church.

In the midst of my private lament, I glanced over at the pile of mail, haphazardly strewn across the front passenger's seat. I needed a break from my internal struggle. Reaching for it, I wanted to feel normal and pretend for a moment that my burdens weren't overtaking me. Silly jewelry catalogs would make me feel normal, and so would perforated pizza coupons. Even insurance statements and power bills would have been strangely soothing, if only because they were familiar.

Sticking out between two legal-size envelopes was a fat, golden-yellow one. I recognized it as a bubble mailer, and it immediately piqued my interest. I was upset, and suddenly here was hope that whatever was inside would make me feel better. What I found inside was intended for that very purpose but instead, for a moment, actually made me feel much worse.

I ripped open the sealed top with my teeth. The top parted to show a delicate box inside, and I lifted it through the opening. It was a beautiful white box featuring the name of an online jewelry store I immediately recognized. Just months before, a ministry I did coordinating work for had placed an order from that company for an online giveaway we were doing. We had purchased a customizable leather cuff with the word *Truth* engraved on the metal plate attached to the top. I loved it so much that I wanted to keep it for myself and said so to my friend LeAnn, the executive director of the ministry. She must have made a mental note of it, because this package was from her.

I reached into the box to pull the beautiful leather

cuff from its bed of cotton. It smelled like new leather, and I could not wait to put it on my wrist. I couldn't believe I had received such a beautiful gift on such a horrible, discouraging day. It was a sweet, sweet moment that came at the perfect time. *Thank You, Lord, for this gift*, I thought. I looked at it appreciatively. But just as I was basking in the moment, my joy wilted as quickly as it had sprung up. As I turned the cuff over, my throat dried out and my heart began to beat a little faster. The inscription on this one's metal plate wasn't *Truth*. It was *Thrive*.

Knowing the name of our church, LeAnn had thoughtfully ordered the bracelet with this custom personalization, just for me. A flood of mixed emotions—of appreciation, love, shame, fear, and guilt—filled my heart as I stared at the bracelet in my hand. I didn't want to see that word or even think about it right now. This should have been a gift I loved, and really, it was. But under the circumstances and with my emotions so conflicted, it was a tangible reminder of how much our attempt to serve God had done nothing but fail.

I clenched my fist, wishing for a punching bag to pound my feelings into, though I knew that wouldn't make them go anywhere. *How could You, God?* I said in my mind. *On today of all days, You let me get this cruel*

*reminder of how horribly we have done things, as if You are
shoving it in my face? Is this some kind of sick joke, or do
You really just not love me and You want me to run away
from You? We failed, okay? What more do You want me to
say? WE FAILED.* The tears had begun to fall again, and
I didn't even try to stop them. I didn't care what anyone
thought now. God had been cruel to me and that was
the lowest rejection I could ever feel. The pain from the
stigma of failure was searing.

As in all of our moments of pain, in this moment,
God heard mine. And right then He spoke to my heart,
gently but firmly. It couldn't have been clearer if He had
embodied my steering wheel and spoken it to my face.

*Lisa, I love you. I know you are hurting right now, and
I know why. But in these months of doing Thrive Church,
have you gotten to know Me better?*

I didn't want to deal with this question, but I knew
I must consider it. He was God, after all. Hearing from
Him was always important, especially after living so
many years hearing absolutely nothing from Him. *Have
I gotten to know Him better?* It didn't take me long to
ponder it. Through all the months of discerning what
move to take and living through the difficulties and
maneuvering the complications, the one thing that had
emerged was a vibrant new way of seeking His face. It
was, more than ever, my daily lifeline. This experience

had driven me to my knees and made me pursue God like never before.

"Yes, Father," I said, barely above a whisper. "I have gotten to know You so much better."

I halfway expected that to be the extent of our conversation. God had made His point: I had grown closer to Him through this experience, difficult as it was. But in the next moment, He spoke to my heart again: *If then you have gotten to know Me better and you were created for that purpose, how can you consider your experience with Thrive Church a failure? It is instead a wild success.*

Instantly, a new truth about the word *thrive* came into perspective—one that had been under my nose but had eluded me for months of my maneuvering with the church. Thrive was not simply the name of the ministry we had started, as I had always believed. Instead, it was a personal call on my life. And that could be answered inside the walls of Thrive Church or outside them. It was a Matthew 22 "love God, love people" perspective that wasn't relegated to any specific work. I could love and serve God anytime, anywhere, in any way that He designed me for. I could thrive if we closed the church tomorrow or the twelfth of never.

That moment forever changed my life. It changed my spiritual vision of what success for the follower of Christ really is: drawing near to the heart of God in the effort to serve Him. It made me understand that the only person who really fails is the one who never attempts anything for God in the first place. It was a gracious new way of seeing things for what they were, and as a most undeserving candidate for insight, I was humbled that God had taught me such a rich lesson in the moment my flesh most threatened to consume me.

I wear my Thrive cuff bracelet almost every day now. The sight of it brings me joy from the memory of an experience that drew me closer to Jesus. It serves as a reminder to this very personal call and the moment God intimately spoke to my heart in a hot, stuffy car in the car line. I wasn't sure I would ever be able to think of the word *thrive* without remembering the difficulties of this experience: asking people you love to believe in you and invest in the ministry you birthed, only to turn around and tell them you are closing the church and you don't want them to follow you anymore. But it is true, and I can only attach it to the enormous love of God who makes us able to open our eyes to truth, even when everything within us wants to shut them tightly.

This is an aspect of wholeness that is most important. When God is allowed to fill up our holes with His wholeness, our once painful or difficult experiences and even our positive experiences are allowed to offer new perspective. We will see things as they are, rather than in a skewed light. We will view things in a new way, in the scope of eternity and through a clearer lens. We will be able to look at our experiences and call them circumstances . . . pages of our journey . . . that, good or bad, did not define us or cause us to become all the things we feared we would. We will be able to see things we tried but didn't continue as things that didn't work out but that we learned from. We will be able to call it an experience I'll never forget but one that doesn't own me.

Experiencing God

About a month before the Thrive leather cuff bracelet incident, I found my husband sitting on the edge of our worn sofa, staring at the floor, late one Saturday night.

"I can't do this anymore," he said, which scared me more than maybe anything else he could have said. He never said it in the early months of the launch, when we endured late nights and logistical complications. He never said it during the many Saturdays the kids and I left him at home to go do something fun while he prepared a message by himself after already working a sixty-hour week at his other job.

It changed my spiritual vision of what success for the follower of Christ really is: drawing near to the heart of God in the effort to serve Him.

Even when people he loved left the church by the handful, he never said it. But for some reason, on this night,
he did. By the look on his face, I feared he meant it.

We had not yet decided to close the church, but
we had become open to the idea that it might need to
happen. But this was Saturday night, and Scotty had
to preach the next morning. He couldn't quit tonight,
though my heart wanted me to tell him he could. I
knew, instead, I would need to be to him the strength he
didn't have, and all I could do at that moment was say
to Jesus silently, *You're gonna have to help me talk him off
this ledge. I've got nothing.*

"It'll be okay, honey," I told him. As the words
escaped my mouth, I knew I didn't mean them. For a
few minutes, I watched him cry. It melted my heart to
see such a man of strength under such duress. After we
talked a few minutes, he gained the strength to go to
bed and wake up to face another Sunday-morning hat
change: wearing the weighty one of being someone's
pastor. That next morning, as I sat on the front row
hearing him preach, I felt a silent knowing between us.
Only the two of us knew that just the night before, this
man who now spoke with such conviction had said he
wanted to quit. It was one of many private emotions that
the two of us would share over the course of the experience and that bonded us in a beautiful new way.

But though the night had come and gone and so had another Sunday, I knew in my heart Scotty was drowning in the pressure of being bivocational, keeping the business from closing, maintaining friendships, and providing leadership for a congregation of people who had pressing needs. I knew he silently feared what gripped me as well: the idea that in the effort to minister to everyone else, we would somehow lose intimacy with our own family. We had seen this happen to people in ministry whom we knew and loved, and they regretted it years later, after their kids were grown. I determined to take him away, just for a night, without asking him if it was okay, knowing how much we both needed it. I arranged for us to go to a place in the mountains that had always been both a refuge and a place we met with God. And so it was, that on the following Thursday I was in the driver's seat of the car, taking us both up to a retreat in the mountains.

Upon arrival, we found our way to the room in the top corner of a massive log-built lodge, far away from the pressures of our world in the city. The large hill we could see behind the lodge beckoned us to come hike it, as we had both done in the past, though never together. After changing our shoes, we ventured out. We made our way up the hill, making small talk but with an air of reverence for the creation that was encasing us like parentheses—trees so tall you could barely see their tops, rocks that led up to a wooden deck replete with cushions to rest on its wooden benches. After what seemed like miles, we walked onto the wooden surface and immediately took to our knees in unison as if our very lives depended on it. More than anything, we were there to meet with God. We had never needed His presence or His wisdom more, and we couldn't afford to waste time.

For two hours on the top of the hill, we prayed. We prayed for strength. We prayed for courage. We asked Him to forgive us if we had missed Him somewhere in the process. We begged Him to help us figure out what to do next. Scotty prayed . . . I prayed . . . we said nothing . . . then we prayed some more. We stained the wood with our tears and indented wood patterns in our knees until we finally slid the cushions under us.

Finally, after hours, we felt completion with our prayers. Without saying a word, Scotty rearranged the cushions for us to lie down on. We flipped to our backs and lay side by side, staring up at the sky. Breaking the silence, Scotty eventually spoke—but not to me. I was just an eavesdropper, listening in on a man's earnest prayers to his God. And this is what he prayed: "God, if You heard us, please give us a sign. Let just one leaf fall from the tree but not another, all the time we are here."

I was surprised to hear my husband pray such an

unsophisticated prayer, yet I knew it was his way of begging God to be real and know our struggle. After the months we had endured emotionally and the two hours we had just spent praying, this felt completely necessary, as if we needed His assurance that we were worth His time even though we had surely disappointed Him. The truth is, I had often asked God to give me signs in other prayers I had prayed throughout my life—maybe never such a tangible, immediate request, but always with the same underlying desire to experience God.

I looked up at the large tree looming over the top of the deck. It was so enormous that the sky overhead was almost completely covered by it, but for a few slivers of luminous baby blue sprinkled throughout its leafy clusters. The day was windy, and the more I looked at the leaves, the more I felt skeptical that God would honor Scotty's request. Doubt had surfaced in my heart once again, this time in the greatest of ironies—in the form of my "practical" encouragement that *Scotty* should not doubt God if it didn't happen.

We lay there looking up at the leafy sky for at least one more minute. It was about that time the wind began to pick up and blow in a strong, wild gust. I braced myself, knowing that it was likely we would be bombarded with falling leaves, and rehearsing in my mind what I might say to encourage my husband to continue trusting that God had heard us anyway. The wind continued to blow hard and strong for a few more seconds before finally settling to stillness. Not a single leaf had fallen off the tree the entire time the wind gusted. I marveled at that for a minute, grateful that at least we weren't covered in leaves, and started to summon my words of encouragement.

Then, unmistakably, and as if magnified in the serenity of the stilled mountain air, it came: one single leaf falling from the tree above us slowly, in such a fanciful way that it seemed to be announcing its presence with a dance. It was so clear, so present, so real that I could not explain it away. A single leaf had fallen, but not another, just as my husband requested. Even in the gusts of wind that came thereafter as we lay there, awestruck, another one never fell. We celebrated His presence with a tearful embrace. We had gotten on our faces before God, and He had heard us.

I've prayed for a lot of things throughout a lot of years, but never before or since have I experienced such a precious, meaningful moment of prayer in all my life. I've had a lot of prayers answered, too, but never quite in that way. I cannot help but believe that the kind of faith that is willing to pray honest, dedicated, outlandish prayers such as Scotty did that day results in a fresh rendering of God's Spirit—in whatever way He chooses to render it. The one thing I know from this experience is that God draws near to the hearts that draw near to Him, and that is not just a truth on paper. Our moment on the hill didn't change the outcome of the church or take away all the pain from the experience. But that day we felt the assurance of His presence with us even so.

Profound spiritual fellowship with God is an amazing benefit of wholeness, and it is felt in the strong presence of God in our lives. Fellowship with God is a beautiful marriage of spirits whereby we are one with God and our partnership reaches a new level of intimacy and knowledge: "God . . . has invited you into partnership with his Son, Jesus Christ our Lord" (1 Corinthians 1:9). To understand that our core purpose on this earth is to be in intimate relationship with God and then to actually be at that place feels like the closest thing to perfection we can experience on this earth. Being filled with holes because of our experiences limits us from this intimacy and unity. But when those holes are filled up by God . . . we are whole. It is a place so sweet that even the most wounded in life are able to say, *I don't prefer my experience, but it was worth journeying through it to know God in this way.*

Seeing the Fruit

I can't imagine anything more natural than wanting to see fruit from the labor of our experiences. But the tough reality is, sometimes we won't. Some of my missionary friends have spent years out in the jungle with minimal spiritual breakthrough in the villages they minister to. Some good friends of our family, church planters, moved into a largely nonbelieving community and spent two years cultivating relationships and sharing with them about God, never to see one single person come to accept Christ. It is in discouraging times like these that we have to rest in the fact that we are God's and that He will use our experiences to be fruitful in someone else's life, even if it isn't our own, for eternity if not for now. He *will* use them . . . we just may never know how. But sometimes, in His timing and great graciousness, He does let us know.

Often the experiences my husband and I had with Thrive Church made us feel like we let people down, and this was a most profound emotion. Sometimes just after the closing, we felt guilty if we experienced any feeling of relief or blessing, especially because we were worried that others did not fare as well from the experience as we did. We wondered if the people we led were now going to church anywhere, and if so, whether this experience had tarnished them on leadership. We wondered if they would ever believe another leader who felt prompted to do something by God. Since we had met for a time on a college campus, we wondered a lot about the many students who had come to Thrive Church expecting a place that would love and care for them while they were away from home. They had made a place in our hearts, and we were afraid we had disappointed them.

Months went by, and we had refrained from contacting those in the church right after the closing to give them an easier break from us as their leaders. So it was with great surprise that I opened my e-mail in-box one day to this message from one of our most faithful college girls at Thrive Church. Alisha's note began with a few pleasantries and then dove right in to become one of the most encouraging notes I've ever received:

I can't imagine anything more natural than wanting to see fruit from the labor of our experiences. But the tough reality is, sometimes we won't.

> *I just wanted to take a couple of minutes and thank you and Mr. Scott for allowing the Lord to use you in so many great ways, one of the smaller ones being to help further my walk and experience the best growth that I have experienced in my twenty years. . . . Even though I was sad to hear that we wouldn't be meeting as a congregation, I had one of those feelings driving to church that morning that*

*we probably wouldn't be meeting much more. The
more I thought about it after the service, the more
I realized how awesome God is. He put me in that
wonderful group of people in a time where I needed
some hard-core and honest learning and growing in
my walk. You and Mr. Scott (and the whole staff
at Thrive), more than anything that was said, helped
me to see what a true believer and follower of Christ
acts and lives like as an adult. I am in that weird
"in-between" stage . . . and when I sat back and
thought about it, your Christian example has popped
up in my mind when I think about my future.
Thanks for a great year at Thrive . . . !*[7]

The words in this message touched my heart in so many
deep places. I was overjoyed to hear from Alisha, yet I
felt even more strongly that I had heard from God. He
knew my heart; He knew I desired a tangible validation
of our time as Thrive Church and what it meant, at
least to someone. To see the fruit of the experience that
brought us many late, difficult nights and stressful days
through the eyes of this young woman was a gift in the
most gracious, sovereign way.

Our Father knows what needs we have, and often
we do need to see fruit from our experiences. As flesh-
and-bone creatures, we have a desire to see things, to feel

them and touch them, which is why faith is so difficult for us. Sometimes we have to soldier on in faith. Though it is difficult to labor without the guarantee of fruit, that cannot be our motive to serve God or we won't last long.

But fruit is something God wants us to enjoy, so when we do experience it, we can consider it a gift: "You will eat the fruit of your labor; blessings and prosperity will be yours" (Psalm 128:2, NIV). Wholeness offers this fruit, because when we are whole, our eyes are opened to see the fruit of our labor and receive it as the gift it is intended to be, without a false sense of humility or an elevation of our involvement. To come from a place of feeling stifled by the limits of the holes from our experiences—those lingering negative feelings or the pride it produced within us or the way it caused us to marginalize God—and go to a place where the blessing of God has no limits is enormously satisfying. Wholeness lets us welcome fruit from the experiences of our life that we never thought we would get through. Our experience of God is enlarged, and the fruit from our other experiences becomes worth its growing pains.

To know God . . . that is the greatest experience we will ever have, either on this earth or in the eternity to come. To get past the definitions our experiences have placed on us and the holes those experiences have produced is true spiritual triumph. To receive from our experiences the benefits of wholeness—God's presence, a new perspective, the fruit manifested in someone else's life, among others—is satisfying and rich. To understand that we do not have to be limited by anything—our failures, our successes, our pain, our injustices—fills our soul with hope and promise, the kind that Jesus says is ours to begin with as children of God ("just as you have been called to one glorious hope for the future," Ephesians 4:4). These are the things that give life to our weary, hole-filled souls. These are the things we get when we reach a place of wholeness— often found by the gritty, desperate prayers of the people who go to the top of the mountain to meet with God . . . or tell Him in the privacy of a quiet room that they will give Him a try . . . or beg Him to give them the strength to wake up from a difficult experience and welcome their breathing. And He arrives, in all of His wholeness, ready to do the filling our holes need.

Questions to Consider

1. Is it possible to know wholeness in your experiences, even the most painful ones? How? Why is it important?

2. What does it mean to you to know that "God is bigger than all our man-made messes"? How can you use that knowledge to gain wholeness from your experiences?

CHAPTER 8

THE WHOLE STORY

In my deepest wound I saw your glory, and it dazzled me.
ST. AUGUSTINE

THE WHOLE STORY. Consuming. Significant. Essential.
I wonder, what is yours?

Whatever it is, it involves Jesus. Without Him, it's
just a story, and a variety of those are told every day.
Some of them are riveting. Others are inconsequential.
Many of them will matter. Most of them won't alter the
course of a life.

But the whole story—now, that is different. It has the
effectiveness to transform hopeless cases. It has the force
to wreck entire trains of thought. It has the potency to
rupture the shell of a rock-solid heart. It has the capacity
to heal a life most broken.

The whole story of Jesus can be told in this one word: *redemption*. The entirety of humanity is held in its singular yet encompassing definition of obedience, sacrifice, and glory. With it, there is completeness. Redemption is the whole story of life, both now and eternal.

As you spend the last few pages of this book thinking about your whole story, I hope you will find yourself eager to allow your future to be impacted by it. Though this chapter closes this book, it does not end your journey. Your story with Jesus on the pages of your journey is one story that will never end.

What Does End

One of the greatest gifts God gave to us was creating our humanness with an end. I do not mean this in a physical sense, though ultimately that is also a gift, of course, because the believer moves on from this life to beautiful, lasting things on a different level of wholeness in heaven. Nor do I mean this in any sort of out-of-body sense. Coming to the end of ourselves happens while we are still very much alive and breathing and still very much a part of this earthly world. It is what happens after our efforts to maneuver, juggle, hurdle, and accomplish don't work in the way we want them to. When we are in a facedown position, not unlike the one my father found himself in on the gravel driveway that day. When life as we have known it no longer works. We come to the "end" of ourselves when we have a contrite heart, one that God can work with. Brokenness within is often the place where wholeness throughout begins.

But we can come to the end of ourselves without a specific moment of brokenness. Coming to the end of ourselves is really about recognizing our lack of human ability to make ourselves well and our need for God to complete us. It is what has to happen before our wholeness with Him can begin. Psalm 51 is one of my favorite passages in all the Bible because it reminds me of the humble, desperate position I need to be in so God can work through me. David, the very king of Israel, found himself in this position before God in his extramarital relationship with Bathsheba. After the prophet Nathan confronted him about his sin, David offered this insight to God in verse 17: "The sacrifice you desire is a broken spirit. You will not reject a broken and repentant heart, O God."

What is it that keeps us from starting down the road toward wholeness? It is not that God turns our contrite hearts away. It's just that we do not always allow ourselves to go to such depth and vulnerability. Instead, we claw and grasp and reach and strain to stay afloat by our own efforts. All the while Jesus wants us to face the end of ourselves so He can fully begin.

The precious reality is this: holes can only be filled by the Holy. When we get to the place where we say, "God, I can't do this life thing without You; I can't try hard enough to make things work; I need You to make me whole so I can experience peace and joy and fullness," that is when His power in our life to fill our every void with His presence and character can be realized. Isaiah 57:15 says it this way: "The high and lofty one who lives in eternity, the Holy One, says this: 'I live in the high and holy place with those whose spirits are contrite and humble. I restore the crushed spirit of the humble and revive the courage of those with repentant hearts.'" To come to the end of ourselves is to welcome a fresh, revitalizing work of Jesus. If you are in that place, you are right where you need to be to be made whole.

Coming to the end of ourselves is about recognizing our lack of human ability to make ourselves well and our need for God to complete us.

Where You Might Be

The Bible is the most compelling place to find parallels to your life—which makes sense, when you consider that it is the inspired Word of God given to show you how to live. In the sense of wholeness, where you are right now (with holes or made whole) is directly related to the aspects of your religion, your roles, and your experiences that have accompanied you on your journey and how you have chosen to respond to them. By now I hope you have recognized those in your own life and have a picture of what a life of wholeness in those areas can look like. What you may not realize is that the stories from the Bible have very deep insight into the chapters you have lived.

The House Built on Sand. You might be the person who has built your life on the ritual of religion, rather than a rich relationship with God. As a result, you have opened yourself up to something that has hurt you or stifled you by its rigid tradition. "But anyone who hears my teaching and doesn't obey it is foolish, like a person who builds a house on sand. When the rains and floods come and the winds beat against that house, it will collapse with a mighty crash" (Matthew 7:26-27). Like the person who built a house on sand, maybe your life is collapsing around you. This happens when our foundation is in a human person or community. No matter how meaningful and important these relationships are, they can never be enough. We weren't meant to worship our religion, so worshiping it will never fulfill us. Instead, it will create holes that cause frustration, pride, doubt, resentment, and worry, and will take the focus off of God. But a foundation built on the person of Jesus will never falter, sink, or become compromised by the elements of this world. This stability is something religion has never been able to accomplish but something your capable Jesus offers to you, whispering to your heart, *Dear child, build your house on Me.*

The Wandering Prodigal. You might be the person who has chosen to leave home in search of something greater, while the identity you actually need, you already have in Jesus. You have been jaded by your role and you have chosen to see yourself in light of the things you do, not who you are. So when the world promises fulfillment but doesn't deliver, you feel cheated. Running after the things you thought you wanted or needed has only resulted in a slow death to your soul. Your identity is in the wrong thing and as a result, the wellness of your life is in constant danger of being weakened by holes of fear, self-reliance, and discouragement. But Jesus wants to welcome you home, just as the prodigal was welcomed home by his father. He beckons you to embrace your completed identity in Him and longs to say of you, "He was lost, but now he is found!" (Luke 15:32).

The Locust-Eaten Life. Perhaps you have weathered difficult experiences, ones that have left you feeling cheated out of life, resentful of things that were not within your control. The locusts of your circumstances have taken time, relationships, and your sense of security and well-being from you. As a result, you live with fear, doubt, anger, resentment, and mistrust, and it consumes you. Or you may have had good experiences that have caused you to trust yourself more than God. In the same way, the locusts from your circumstances have eaten holes of pride and self-dependence within you. But Jesus allows your experiences for a greater purpose—that you might know wholeness in Him. His great promise to you is that of Joel 2:25, "I will give you back what you lost to the swarming locusts."

No matter where you might be, you are not out of the reach of God. There is great movement from Him in your direction. There is no one who wants you to become whole more than Jesus, as He says in John 10:10: "I have come that [you] may have life, and have it to the full" (NIV). He just wants you to stop trying to find other sources to do what only He can.

Jesus, the Protagonist

If you ever doubt what Jesus can do in your life, read Matthew 8 and 9. I have just come off diving into these two chapters, and I am reminded of the amazing spiritual and physical phenomena Jesus enacted in the lives of everyday people who asked Him to help them. I'm also reminded of the spiritual place from which many people traveled in order to get to Jesus and receive His healing.

Matthew 8 opens up with Jesus and a buzz. Crowds of excited people had begun to gather to hear His teaching, and what they heard amazed them (7:28). In the midst of the large gathering, what I can only picture as a gnarly looking man pushed his way forward to approach the teacher, Jesus. A horrific, highly contagious disease called leprosy visibly compromised the man, likely causing him to be exiled—both in his body and in his spirit—by the people in his community. If I close my eyes I can almost see the revulsion on the faces of the people he brushed past, as they bristled at the thought that he might have touched them. They may have even gasped out loud, which he would have barely noticed, as he was undoubtedly used to this reaction and was unwavering in his single focus to get to Jesus. His request to Jesus was a paradox of sorts—a simple request of maybe the greatest complexity: to make him well. In that moment Jesus fully embodied graciousness, responding to the man in the most beautiful three words he had likely ever heard: "I am willing" (Matthew 8:3). I can only imagine the healing that swept over the diseased man's soul at that compassionate acknowledgment from Jesus.

I am willing. These three words spoken over the man with leprosy sum up God's heart for your internal wellness: a place called whole that for much of your life may have eluded you. He wants nothing more than for you to become whole, because He knows what that will mean to your story. You will experience the fullness of living with profound spiritual fellowship, and you will be able to share that with others, representing Him well. The desire of your heavenly Father is that you would know His grace, love, purpose, joy, peace, fulfillment, wisdom, and strength to an extent that our human minds cannot even comprehend and then that you would offer them to others. Just as He offered opportunity and hope to a once-desperate man eaten away by a debilitating disease, He offers us an abundance of these healing gifts to fill the holes that eat away at us.

The man with leprosy had something in common with the other people Jesus healed in this Matthew 8 and 9 passage: they believed in His power, going forward in faith that He would perform it in their lives to make them well. Friends of a paralyzed man brought him to Jesus on a mat and took great pains to position him in front of Jesus for His healing touch (9:1-8). A woman who had been bleeding for twelve years reached out and touched Him (9:19-22). In each case, those involved recognized the movement they needed to make in order to receive His healing. They were willing to risk something in order to reach Jesus, simply because they knew their very lives depended upon it.

The whole story—the story of wholeness—is different from any other story we may ever hear, tell, or know, because it centers around Jesus. In it, He is the divine protagonist—not you or me—and the circumstances of life, the things we have experienced in our religion and with our roles, are mere events along the way in the story of our life. Jesus is central to our whole story because He is the only One who can make us well and complete. Without Him, we have only an earthly story to tell.

Never doubt that your heavenly Father, the protagonist in your story, wants to make you whole and well. I pray that you have already experienced wholeness in salvation, an extravagant gift that cannot be taken away. But life happens, and in our humanity we allow holes to accompany us on our journey. So even though we don't become "born again" *again*, there may indeed be multiple times when we need Him to make us whole. Some of you have resonated with the message of this book because you are a living, breathing testimony of a life made whole by the power of God. You are already sharing your whole story because it burns within you, compelling your voice and life to speak. Some of you have not yet become whole, so you cannot yet share your whole story. But you want to. Please know that you share that desire with your Savior.

The sweetest aspect of this story is the message of

Jesus, the healer, who is willing to make us whole. His desire for you is wellness. His dream for you is wholeness. His heart for you is that you will hear His offer, feel the need, and determine to begin the process.

Your Whole Story

Your story, what happens between you and Jesus on the pages of your journey, is a story of wholeness—your *whole story*.

Your mistakes aren't what's most important—your sins, your missteps, your lost opportunities, your places of pain, your letdowns and injustices, your choices that didn't work out, the things that you couldn't control or didn't choose but happened anyway. Those hold significance only because they show your inability to complete yourself, which was God's design. In the same way, the holes that these things produce are only significant because they display in great contrast the beauty of wholeness through the sufficiency of Jesus. So holes actually help us adore Jesus for putting us in a place where we are no longer limited by them. As it should be with all of life, it all points back to Him.

But though Jesus is the main character in our whole story, He is not its only significant one. You and I are a significant part of our own stories, and the extent to which He is able to make us well within depends on how much we crave, accept, and press in to His willing offer. We have to desire to be made whole in the places that limit us—desire it so much that we will do what it takes to have it. Do you have that kind of desire? If you do, you are heading down the path toward wholeness.

It is possible to be a believer and not have the kind of intimacy with God that He offers. Wholeness—the wellness of our soul from the healing of Jesus—produces profound fellowship with Him, in a way like we may never have known. Do you want that kind of relationship with God? If so, then your desire can propel you. The desire to experience God more than we desire anything else produces in us the attitude of Psalm 142:5: "You are all I really want in life."

How do you become whole? That verse gives the answer. You have to want it. You have to be ready. You have to be tired of living life with holes. You have to realize that there are no shortcuts or formulas, quick fixes or ready-made answers. And then you have to get facedown before God—asking Him to fill you up with His power and life, to heal your insufficiencies and make you well and whole. You have to dig into the Word for yourself and ask Him to reveal Himself to you in a way that blows your mind. And then you have to continue. To stay committed. To stoke your desire by pursuing God and practicing truth. Eventually, the more you press in to Him, the more

He will fill you with Himself. At that point, taking the step to press in to Him will no longer take effort.

And as the world threatens to whisk you away from this new way of living, there are things you have to remember about your journey without Jesus: the things you tried that didn't work, the lack of fulfillment, the stifling of your purpose, the frustrations from knowing God but never really experiencing Him. Remember your religious house built on sand. Remember your prodigal story. Remember the locust-ridden years of your experiences. These are what will remind you, when you are tempted to go back to your holes, that wholeness is worth it.

Holes are only significant because they display the beauty of wholeness through the sufficiency of Jesus.

At the very beginning of this journey, in chapter 1, I showed you the passage in Matthew 13 where Jesus answers the question from His disciples, "Why do you tell stories?" (verse 10, *The Message*). He talks about the importance of them, how they "create readiness, to nudge the people toward receptive insight" (verse 13, *The Message*). But there is another element to the importance of stories, and it involves us. It is found in verse 16, where Jesus says, "Blessed are your eyes, because they see; and your ears, because they hear." We are the receivers of much truth, and because of that we have spiritual eyes that can see and spiritual ears that can hear. With this beautiful capability comes the responsibility of decision. I know sometimes we are afraid to change. More than growth, we fear what things growth and change will require of us. But when we do something that we fear, it alters us, and we find courage to do more. That is what Jesus fashioned us for: to crave the bold, revolutionary life—the one that we were created to live without limits, through His power in our lives.

My friend, this is your moment to do something important. It is your moment to crave a change from Jesus. It is your moment to choose the thing that makes your soul well. It is the moment to discover your whole story. It is your moment to thrive.

Let your eyes see. Let your ears hear. Let your soul be open. Let your mind be renewed. Let your knees wear out from prayer. Let your service to God become grittier. Let your Bible be your oxygen. Let your heart be contrite. Let grace become your name. Let your dam break with tears. Let your spiritual accessories fall away. Let your face writhe in gravel. Let your spirit soar in freedom, as "the God of hope fill[s] you with all joy and peace as you trust in him, so that you may overflow with hope by the power of the Holy Spirit" (Romans 15:13, NIV).

And as you do, let yourself fall into the arms of your perfect, loving Father, who is willing to make you well, ready to make you complete, compelling you to share your whole story.

Questions to Consider

1. Have you ever come to the end of yourself, defined in this chapter as "recognizing our lack of human ability to make ourselves well and our need for God to complete us"? If not, why not? If so, how has that changed your life?

2. Do you recognize yourself in one of the three Bible story applications in this chapter (house built on sand, wandering prodigal, locust-eaten life)? Which one? How can you become whole in that area?

Join the community of those
who are telling their whole story.
Visit us online at
www.lisawhittle.com/thewholestory/
for a downloadable guide to getting started
telling your whole story, too.

Acknowledgments

I can't adequately express all that is in my heart for those who have been my strongest supporters during this grueling writing project. This is my humble attempt at thanking you.

My husband, Scott: Your unique ability to be enormously talented and yet humble enough to serve as an arm lifter to me and others inspires me. Thank you for allowing me to feel safe being myself and teaching me to drink in life more fully. I love only Jesus more than you.

My children, Graham, Micah, and Shae: your lives are my joy. I always wanted to be a mom, but I had no idea what treasures you would be. I adore you.

My parents, Jim and Kathie Reimer: No two people know more about faith than you. Thank you for trusting me with your story. I love you fiercely.

My mentor, Monty: I am awed by your ability to always ask the right questions. Thank you for teaching me about Jesus through your life and for letting me quote you, often.

My circle of closest friends, Colleen, Wendy, Dena: I am better because you are in my life. Thank you for seeing the best in me and being trustworthy girlfriends.

My friend Shawna: you are an amazing listener and advocate. I'll never stop thanking God for our divine connection.

My friends at She Seeks and at Proverbs 31: Thank you for your support and love. I find you all enormously gifted.

My online community of friends: your input matters to me more than you know. Your encouraging words have, many times, convinced me to keep being vulnerable with mine.

My literary agent, Esther Fedorkevich: you are one tenacious woman. Thank you for believing in me and fighting for this book. I won't ever forget your heart to move it forward.

My colleagues and respected friends on this project: David Kinnaman, for using your voice to help champion this book. Jim Henderson, for being the kind of guy who takes the time. You are both rare finds.

My friends at Tyndale House: I'm blessed by what quality, Jesus-loving people you are. You are the real deal, and I'm honored to be in your company.

My editor, Cara Peterson, who has worked tirelessly alongside me on this project. My friend, you have made this book sing. Thank you for letting me see the reader through your eyes. I'm both a fan and a friend, for life.

The incredible George Barna, for being a bold voice for the church, writing a book that inspired this one, and saying yes when you could have said no.

My Jesus: there are no adequate words. You are my whole life.

Appendix

As a lifelong studier of people, I have come to this conclusion: at the core we are all very much the same. Our longings, our fears, our self-doubt, our holes . . . are often universal. Yet many of us feel like we are alone—the only one who feels this way, the only one who struggles, the only one who doesn't have it all together. Hence, my foremost appreciation for this research is because of the concrete way it shows that no one is really alone.

The research for this book, conducted by Barna Research in 2010, taught me yet another important lesson in humanity: we are not always predictable. The way we answer questions—our ability to be completely honest, especially with ourselves—varies, depending upon many things. Some of the answers to the questions I asked, I expected. Others I did not. Many I questioned (to put it mildly). As I wrote the book I considered pushing back on some of these findings, to fit the research into my theories, assessments, and assumptions in an effort to make a point. But in the end I decided that sometimes it's better to simply start a conversation about something important. Here I have simply presented the research in its summarized form so you can form your own conclusions.

You should know that when I began this journey, there were many things that looked different—my circumstances, my belief about where the message would take me, the audience I intended to write for (solely women). But as the project progressed, God changed things. As I opened myself up to His movement, I opened my heart to His plans: I would write this book for the believer, not to a specific gender. I would ask different questions. I would come at the book from my failures, not my successes. All of those nudges, and more, proved to be divine in my life, and I pray that you will see this same divine influence in yours as well.

Here are some of the questions this book first sought to answer and the answers of 603 women to them. The study was done of those eighteen or older who describe themselves as Christians and have attended a Christian church service within the past six months, excluding holiday services or special events. You might not sit among those asked, but you most certainly sit among their community. For as a person, a believer, a person with a voice . . . you are from the same sovereign Source. Truly, we are not alone.

Self-perception

36% see themselves as leaders
49% see themselves as servants
65% see themselves as being deeply spiritual
74% see themselves as being mature in faith

Settings in which self-described leaders provide leadership

52% at a church
28% in the community or neighborhood
31% on the job
13% in a nonprofit organization
29% as a parent or in the home
18% in a school setting

Single most important goal

32% family-oriented
26% faith-oriented
6% health-oriented
5% career-oriented
4% lifestyle-oriented
4% personal growth
4% morality-oriented
3% financial
2% marriage-oriented
1% personal appearance
1% relational
1% travel-oriented
2% have no goals

Single biggest disappointment or emotional hurt in one's life

29% death of a loved one
20% family/children
9% divorce, bad marriage
5% health
4% relational
3% financial
3% morality
2% career
2% faith-oriented
9% no disappointments

Single highest priority in one's life currently

53% family
16% faith
9% health
5% occupational performance
5% lifestyle
3% friends
2% achieving success
2% financial
1% influence
1% leisure

How much influence these have on one's decisions

	A lot	Some	Little
husband's opinions	63%	30%	6%
(base: currently married)			
principles taught in sermons	51%	39%	10%
ideas provided in the media	5%	25%	70%
principles in the Bible	75%	20%	5%
ideas learned from classes/seminars	18%	47%	33%
friends' opinions	10%	51%	38%
information learned from books	27%	51%	22%

How often time is intentionally taken to evaluate the quality of one's relationship with God

3% once or twice a year
5% once every three or four months
10% once every month or two
12% every week
17% several times each week
52% every day

Description of relationship with God

38% extremely close
43% pretty close
17% sometimes close; other times not close
1% either usually not too close or extremely distant

Most important role filled in life

62% parent
13% follower of Christ
11% wife
3% employee or executive
2% church member
2% friend or neighbor
1% American citizen
1% teacher
1% caregiver

Level of satisfaction with aspects of life

	Completely	Mostly	Less
marriage *(base: currently married)*	59%	26%	14%
personal spiritual development	36%	42%	23%
service to people in the community	26%	32%	40%
involvement in church	39%	31%	30%
career or job *(base: currently employed)*	37%	35%	27%
raising of children *(base: have children)*	51%	37%	12%
personal relationships other than family	39%	42%	19%
use of gifts and abilities	31%	38%	30%

Attitudes and behaviors struggled with

	Constantly or often	Sometimes	Not often
anger	5%	31%	65%
selfishness	3%	22%	74%
envy or jealousy	1%	12%	86%
lust	3%	5%	91%
arrogance	2%	14%	83%
excessive quarreling or arguing	4%	15%	81%
inefficiency	8%	34%	57%
disorganization	15%	35%	49%

Evident spiritual qualities

	A lot	Some	Not much or not at all
joy	73%	24%	3%
spiritual freedom	72%	21%	3%
fear	3%	26%	71%
doubt	3%	25%	71%
confusion	3%	26%	71%
fulfillment	67%	26%	6%

Intentional service for God

46% pray for others
24% encourage people
24% help needy/disadvantaged/homeless people
23% talk about Jesus/gospel with people
21% volunteer at church
17% donate money to religious causes
 9% volunteer at nonprofit/service organization
 8% teach a religious class
 8% provide leadership to a group
 3% personal discipleship activities
13% no intentional service

Things that hold one back from service

26% lack of opportunities
12% not sure what to do
11% too busy/no time
 7% laziness/selfishness
 7% haven't thought about it
 6% health issues/disability/old age
 5% no resources
 4% fear of failure
 4% other commitments/job
 3% family obligations

General conclusions

A total of 83% say they are capable of doing more to serve God.

Of those, 87% say they should be doing more to serve God.

That represents 73% of all respondents who feel they can and should be doing more to serve God.

Notes

1. Taken from OmniPoll 2011, an omnibus survey of 1,014 adults from across the nation conducted by The Barna Group in April 2011.
2. From OmniPoll 2011.
3. Stephen Mansfield, *ReChurch: Healing Your Way Back to the People of God* (Carol Stream, IL: Tyndale House Publishers, 2010), 45.
4. Eric Metaxas, *Bonhoeffer: Pastor, Martyr, Prophet, Spy* (Nashville, TN: Thomas Nelson, 2010), 187.
5. George Barna, *Revolution* (Carol Stream, IL: Tyndale House Publishers, 2006), 186.
6. You can find out more about SOME Ministries, dedicated to reaching lost and unchurched men for Christ, at http://www.wow-whitetails.com.
7. Printed with Alisha's permission.

About the Author

LISA WHITTLE is the author of three books, including her latest with Tyndale's Barna imprint. A fresh, bold voice in the Christian community, she is a speaker, ministry leader, and pastor's daughter with deep roots in the church. Her past experiences include writing stints with Catalyst and Women of Faith, church planting, national media appearances, and traveling with Compassion International. She speaks to audiences across the United States, inspiring conversation about wholeness by the transparent sharing of her own story. Lisa, a wife and a mother of three, resides in North Carolina. Visit her online at www.lisawhittle.com.

Barna Books encourage and resource committed believers seeking lives of vibrant faith—and call the church to a new understanding of what it means to be the Church.

For more information, visit www.tyndale.com/barnabooks.

BARNA

Online Discussion *guide*

Tᴀᴋᴇ *your* Tʏɴᴅᴀʟᴇ ʀᴇᴀᴅɪɴɢ
ᴇxᴘᴇʀɪᴇɴᴄᴇ *to the* ɴᴇxᴛ ʟᴇᴠᴇʟ

A FREE discussion guide for this book
is available at bookclubhub.net, perfect
for sparking conversations in your book
group or for digging deeper into the text
on your own.

www.bookclubhub.net

*You'll also find free discussion guides for
other Tyndale books, e-newsletters, e-mail
devotionals, virtual book tours, and more!*